Sophocles: Elect

DUCKWORTH COMPANIONS
TO GREEK AND ROMAN TRAGEDY

Series editor: Thomas Harrison

Also available

Euripides: Hippolytus
Sophie Mills

Euripides: Medea
William Allan

Seneca: Phaedra
Roland Mayer

Seneca: Thyestes
P.J. Davis

Sophocles: Ajax
Jon Hesk

Sophocles: Women of Trachis
Brad Levett

DUCKWORTH COMPANIONS
TO GREEK AND ROMAN TRAGEDY

Sophocles: Electra

Michael Lloyd

Duckworth

First published in 2005 by
Gerald Duckworth & Co. Ltd.
90-93 Cowcross Street, London EC1M 6BF
Tel: 020 7490 7300
Fax: 020 7490 0080
inquiries@duckworth-publishers.co.uk
www.ducknet.co.uk

A catalogue record for this book is available
from the British Library

ISBN 0 7156 3303 1

Typeset by Ray Davies
Printed and bound in Great Britain by
Biddles Ltd, King's Lynn, Norfolk

Contents

To the memory of my mother
Jean Beryl Lloyd, 1924-2004

References

Books and articles listed in the Guide to Further Reading on pp. 147-50 are cited by author's name and page number (e.g. 'Stinton, p. 469'). No attempt has been made to give a comprehensive account of scholarly views on every issue in *Electra*. The Guide to Further Reading offers some information about the abundant secondary literature on the play.

Translations from ancient and modern authors are, unless otherwise indicated, my own.

1

Sophocles and his Theatre

The Festival of Dionysus in Athens

Tragedy was a distinctively Athenian genre, and in Sophocles' lifetime the great majority of tragedies were written by Athenians and produced for the first time in Athens. Drama could only be seen there at festivals, the main one for this purpose being the City (or 'Great') Dionysia in late March. Sir Arthur Pickard-Cambridge gives a memorable account of it:

> The importance of the festival was derived not only from the performances of dramatic and lyric poetry but from the fact that it was open to the whole Hellenic world and was an effective advertisement of the wealth and power and public spirit of Athens, no less than of the artistic and literary leadership of her sons. By the end of March the winter was over, the seas were navigable, and strangers came to Athens from all parts for business or pleasure.[1]

There was a public holiday, honours were proclaimed, prisoners were released on bail, and there were patriotic ceremonies in the theatre itself. The festival seems to have been instituted or reorganized under the régime of the tyrant Pisistratus, who ruled Athens on and off from 561 to 527 BC. The word 'tyrant' in Greek history refers to a sole ruler, with no implication that he was especially oppressive. This was in fact a period of growing prosperity in Athens, associated with public works and flourishing artistic activity.

Thespis was the first to win a prize for tragedy at the festival, and was traditionally credited with having invented the genre

9

(*c.* 534 BC). He introduced speeches into what had previously been a purely choral performance, and presumably engaged in some dialogue with the chorus. He used masks and other forms of facial disguise, so there would have been an element of impersonation in his performance. Instead of telling a story, he enacted it. Much remains speculative, and it should be stressed that the origin of tragedy is one of the most contentious topics in the whole of classical scholarship. The official list of victors in the city archives seems to have gone back no further than 502/1 BC, and some recent scholars have argued that this was the date of the institution of tragedy at the festival. It would thus follow shortly after the beginning of democracy in Athens (508/7 BC), conveniently for those who believe that tragedy had a specifically democratic character.[2]

Dionysus, in whose honour the festival was held, was principally the god of wine and intoxication. He was also the god of ecstasy and madness more generally, and the results of this could be destructive as well as beneficial. His followers in myth include the maenads, women who break out from the confinement of their homes and dance frenziedly across the mountainside. Dionysus and his worship are vividly portrayed in Euripides' *Bacchae* (405 BC), but this is a rare example of the god of the festival appearing as a character in the plays performed there. His realm can be summarized as the abandonment of everyday identity and the submergence of the self in something larger. This is a plausible, if somewhat abstract, explanation for his patronage of drama. Masks were associated with his worship from an early date, and this no doubt contributed to their use in drama.[3]

The City Dionysia included processions and sacrifices, but was unique for its five days of choral and dramatic poetry. On the first day there were dithyrambs. The dithyramb was a dance and song for a chorus of fifty. A chorus of boys and a chorus of men were entered by each of the ten tribes into which the Athenian citizenry had been divided when the democracy was instituted in 508/7 BC. Dithyrambs survive only in fragments (i.e. portions preserved on papyrus or quoted by other authors). The second day of the festival was for the comic poets, and normally five of them would contribute one comedy each. The greatest comic dramatist of the fifth century was Aristophanes (*c.* 447 – *c.* 385 BC), eleven of whose plays survive. On each of the next three days, a single tragedian held the stage. Each poet entered three tragedies and a satyr-play. The tragedies could be entirely separate plays, or they could form a connected trilogy on the same subject (like Aeschylus' *Oresteia*). The satyr-play was a mythological burlesque featuring a chorus of satyrs, half-human and half-animal followers of Dionysus. Euripides' *Cyclops* is the only satyr-play to have survived intact, although we have substantial fragments of Sophocles' *Ichneutae* (*Trackers*). The festival was competitive, with a jury selecting winners in tragedy and in comedy. The jury appears to have been open to influence by the reaction of the audience (cf. Csapo and Slater, pp. 157-65). There was also a prize for the best tragic actor from 449 BC, recognizing a growing interest in the contribution of the performer, which could include virtuosity in singing.

The playwrights for each festival were selected ('granted a chorus') by the eponymous archon, the official who gave his name to the Athenian year in which he served. The chorus itself was financed by a wealthy citizen, who could expect to gain prestige and political influence from performing such a public benefaction ('liturgy'). The cost of the actors and their costumes seems to have been borne by the state. The festival took place in the Theatre of Dionysus on the south-east slope of the Acropolis. This was a large open-air venue (holding about 15,000 spectators), located in the very centre of the city. The audience was not restricted to Athenian male citizens, but they would have been in the majority. The evidence suggests that not only resident aliens ('metics') and foreigners could attend, but also slaves, women, and children (see Csapo and Slater, pp. 286-305). The significance of these categories as a presence in the audience remains open to debate.[4] At any rate, during Sophocles' career there would have been a substantial proportion of the entire male citizen body (of perhaps 30,000-40,000) present in the theatre. This made it a larger gathering than the assembly, which could only accommodate around 6,000 citizens. The theatre and the assembly, like the lawcourts, were major civic events, at which verbal performances of various kinds could be listened to and assessed.[5]

The Athenian theatre

The Theatre of Dionysus was not a permanent stone building until the later fourth century. The *skênê* (stage-building) in Sophocles' day was a wooden structure with a large central door, erected for each festival on a stone foundation. It represents a palace in four of Sophocles' extant plays (including *Electra*), and in the other three a tent, a cave, and a grove. Sophocles introduced scene-painting, no doubt on panels which could be attached to the front of the *skênê* for each play. The area in front of the *skênê* where the actors performed (hereinafter 'the stage') would have been raised, if at all, by no more than a foot or two. There was easy communication with the *orchêstra*, where the chorus danced and sang. The *orchêstra* was probably circular in the fifth century, but the matter is disputed (see Csapo and Slater, pp. 79-88). The audience sat on wooden planks or benches on the hillside above. The acting area was large and open, and entrances and exits were major events. The stage was free of naturalistic clutter, so that every stage property would have made a distinct contribution to the visual meaning of the play. One piece of stage machinery which was used in *Electra* was the *ekkyklêma*. This was a wheeled trolley which could be rolled out of the central door of the *skênê*. Anything on the *ekkyklêma* was imagined to be inside, although the convention was not always rigidly maintained and characters can start behaving as if they were outside.[6]

Sophocles, for unknown reasons, increased the number of performers in the tragic chorus from twelve to fifteen. The main contribution of the chorus was to sing the odes which effectively divide a play into acts. Sometimes it engages in lyric dialogue

12

with an actor. All these sung passages were accompanied by a musician playing the *aulos*, a reed instrument with two pipes. The chorus leader occasionally makes short interventions in the dialogue, usually of a fairly routine nature. Sophocles also increased the number of speaking actors used in tragedy from two to three (Aristotle, *Poetics* 1449a18-19). He must have made this change early in his career, since Aeschylus adopted it in the *Oresteia*. Each actor could take several parts, sometimes of a widely contrasting nature, and there was no limit to the number of (non-speaking) extras that could be used. All the performers were male. The chorus and the actors wore full-face masks with wigs. None survives, but vase-paintings reveal them to have been basically naturalistic in the fifth century, and not grotesque or distorted like the masks of some later periods (see Simon, pp. 10-11, with plate 4).

All surviving tragedies, with the exception of Aeschylus' *Persians*, take their subject matter from myth.[7] The myths may have been well-known, but the dramatists still had plenty of room for manoeuvre. Some elements may have been fixed (e.g. that Orestes kills Clytemnestra), but others left scope for adaptation or even invention. The use of myth meant that tragedy was not dealing in any direct way with contemporary life. Few extant tragedies are set in the territory of Athens, and only one (Aeschylus' *Eumenides*) in the city itself. The myths are set in the distant past. The characters of tragedy are often royal, although in real life the Athenians abhorred the very idea of tyranny.[8] Foreigners and slaves are prominent. Women play a much larger role than they did in Athenian public life, but it would be mistaken to assess their behaviour in tragedy purely in terms of what was conventionally appropriate in fifth-century Athens. The world of tragedy is decidedly 'other' from the point of view of the Athenian male citizen, and its relevance to contemporary life is indirect and oblique. Recent scholarship has stressed that the subject matter of tragedy is 'not here, not now, not us'.[9]

Sophocles

The only continuous ancient account of Sophocles' life is the brief *Life of Sophocles*, which seems to have been written in the late second century BC and is included in some of the mediaeval manuscripts of his plays. These lives of poets contain some facts which can be verified, others which seem plausible enough, and a good deal of fiction derived from their works or from jokes in comedy.[10] Another source is the Byzantine encyclopaedia called the *Suda* (*c.* AD 1000), which preserves much valuable information from antiquity. Otherwise, we have a couple of inscriptions and a handful of references in ancient authors.

Sophocles was born *c.* 496 BC at Colonus, just over a mile north of the walls of Athens and two miles from the Acropolis. The rural beauty of the place is vividly conveyed in his last play *Oedipus at Colonus*. He led a victory song after the battle of Salamis (480 BC), 'carrying a lyre, naked, and anointed with oil' (*Life* 4). He competed at the City Dionysia for the first time in 468 BC, when he was victorious and defeated the old master Aeschylus. This was the first of his eighteen victories at the City Dionysia (i.e. with a total of seventy-two plays). He won a few other victories at the Lenaea, a festival which took place in January and had less prestige for tragedy than for comedy. He wrote a total of around one hundred and twenty plays, seven of which survive, and was never placed lower than second. He was thus by far the most successful fifth-century tragedian.

Some details are preserved of Sophocles' career outside the theatre. He was *hellenotamias*, one of the ten treasurers of the Athenian empire, in 443/2 BC. He served, along with Pericles, as one of the ten generals in 441/0 BC, when he took part in the suppression of the revolt of Samos (cf. Thucydides 1.115–17; Plutarch *Pericles* 24-8). He was prominent in Athenian religious life, and allegedly received the cult of the healing god Asclepius into Athens in 420 BC. He consequently received hero-cult himself after his death, under the name Dexion ('The Receiver').[11] He was a member of the standing committee of ten, presumably senior and trusted men, appointed to give advice in the crisis after the Sicilian disaster in 413 BC (cf. Thucydides 8.1). He was thus implicated in the subsequent establishment of the oligarchy of the Four Hundred (411 BC), but argued that there was no better alternative (Aristotle *Rhetoric* 1419a25-30). No harm seems to have been done to his reputation, since he was yet again victorious at the City Dionysia of 409 BC, when *Philoctetes* was one of the successful plays.

Sophocles died sometime between the City Dionysia of 406 BC, when he and his performers marked the recent death of Euripides, and the Lenaea of 405 BC, when he is referred to in Aristophanes' *Frogs* as no longer alive. He won a posthumous victory with the extant *Oedipus at Colonus* in 401 BC, the production no doubt delayed by the final defeat of Athens in the Peloponnesian War (April 404 BC) and the subsequent reign of terror of the Thirty Tyrants (404-3 BC).

Aristophanes famously referred to Sophocles as *eukolos* (contented, good-natured, easy-going), and imagined him continuing to behave in a polite and obliging fashion in the underworld (*Frogs* 82, 786–90). Plato (c. 429-347 BC) has an account of him as an old man being asked whether he was still capable of having sex with a woman. He replied that he was delighted to have escaped from sexual desire, like a slave who has run away from a savage and frenzied master. The story shows that someone who is *eukolos* will not find old age a burden, and also illustrates the witty use of an apt comparison which was the mark of a good conversationalist (*Republic* 329b-d). The merit of Sophocles' contentment in old age is highlighted by the anecdotes about his sexual exploits when he was younger. One such is retailed at some length in a fragment of the memoirs of Ion of Chios (c. 480 – c. 421 BC), which also suggests that his social skills were more notable than his generalship.

These stories give the agreeable impression of a versatile and successful man, whose life coincided with the golden age of Athens, and about whom hardly a bad word was said. They may or may not be literally true, but their principal function is to define Sophocles' literary achievement in terms of his personality and behaviour. Aristophanes' *Frogs* characterizes Aeschylus and Euripides in exactly this way. The idea is that Sophocles' plays were very popular, so he must have been well-liked as an individual. His plays were seen as classic examples of fifth-century tragedy, neither primitive nor decadent, so their author must himself have been urbane and contented. Euripides' plays seemed by contrast subversive, and his character was therefore defined as discontented and misanthropic. This naïve approach to literary biography is generally harmless enough, but can become dangerously circular. A sentimental and idealizing view of Sophocles became prevalent during the nineteenth century, with the result that his plays could be interpreted in the light of an impression of his personality which was itself derived from a particular interpretation of the plays. A famous example is Matthew Arnold's sonnet 'To a friend' (1849), in which the mellow Sophocles, with his 'even-balanced soul', was neither dull nor wild but 'saw life steadily, and saw it whole'. We should not forget that Sophocles' plays contain madness, suicide, parricide, incest, hatred within the family, self-mutilation, despair, and premature death.[12]

The date of *Electra*

Philoctetes (409 BC) and *Oedipus at Colonus* (401 BC) are the only two of Sophocles' seven surviving plays whose exact dates are known. There is some ancient evidence that he was elected general in 441/0 BC on the strength of the success of *Antigone*, and that the play should therefore be dated to *c.* 442 BC, but such anecdotes should be treated with caution. Scholars differ in their willingness to believe that the story would not have gained currency if *Antigone* were not known to have been produced around this time. The plague which opens *Oedipus the King* is sometimes thought to have been influenced by the great plague at Athens (430-26 BC). We must otherwise rely on considerations of style. This is inevitably somewhat subjective, especially as we have only seven out of the ninety or so tragedies which Sophocles wrote in his career. In particular, it is possible that we have no plays from the earliest part of his career. Nevertheless, there is broad agreement that *Ajax* and *Women of Trachis* are relatively early, and probably earlier than *Antigone.*

Electra is generally believed to be no more than ten years earlier than *Philoctetes*, i.e. to belong to the 410s BC. One reason for this belief is the striking similarity in the outline of the two plays. Both plays involve two men, one young and one older, arriving in a place where the main character (Electra, Philoctetes) has been living in torment for many years. The younger man (Orestes, Neoptolemus) is an ephebe, i.e. a youth at the point of transition between childhood and adulthood (approximately between the ages of eighteen and twenty), and he lives as yet in the shadow of a dead father (Agamemnon, Achilles). The newcomers hatch an elaborate plot, which causes yet more suffering to the main character, before recognition and release finally come.

Jebb (pp. lvi-lviii) lists some technical considerations why *Electra* should be considered a late play. The earlier plays have more set speeches, while the later ones prefer rapid and flexible dialogue. *Electra* thus has twenty-five examples of *antilabê*, i.e. division of a line between two speakers, which contributes to the flexibility of the dialogue. There are twenty-two examples in *Philoctetes* and fifty-two in *Oedipus at Colonus*, but no more than ten in any of Sophocles' other plays. *Electra* also has a rare example of a line with more than one change of speaker (1502); there are four examples in *Philoctetes* and one in *Oedipus at Colonus*, but none in any of his other plays. Another late feature of the play is that there is more singing by the leading actor, and less by the chorus alone, than in earlier plays (e.g. *Antigone*). Finally, *Electra* has some striking similarities to the later plays of Euripides, by which Sophocles may indeed have been influenced. These similarities are discussed in Chapter 3, and include the *parodos* (121-250), the agon (516-659), and the recognition duo (1232-87). That is not to say that Sophocles' *Electra* was influenced by Euripides' *Electra* in particular. We have quite reliable technical criteria for dating Euripides' plays, according to which the earliest likely date for his *Electra* is 422 BC and the latest 417 BC (cf. Chapter 2). It is thus marginally more likely that Euripides' *Electra* came before Sophocles', but certainty on the matter is impossible.

2

The Story before Sophocles

Orestes' revenge for the murder of Agamemnon by Clytemnestra and her lover Aegisthus is one of the key events in Greek myth, and was frequently represented in both literature and art. The characters and issues in *Electra* have a long and complex history which is relevant to the interpretation of Sophocles' play. Any adequate response to it must take account of this weight of tradition. Sophocles was free to adapt the story in his own way, but his alterations and omissions are inevitably significant.

Homer

The only reference to Orestes in the *Iliad* is when Agamemnon proposes to compensate Achilles (9.141-7 ≈ 283-9). He promises to honour him as much as his son Orestes, and to give him one of his three daughters in marriage. These daughters are named as Chrysothemis, Laodice and Iphianassa. Their names signify concepts associated with the good king: Golden Law, Justice of the People, and Ruling by Might. We have no way of knowing if Homer has invented or adapted any of these names to suit the context, but they are certainly in keeping with the grandiose tone of Agamemnon's offer. There is no mention of Electra or Iphigenia. There may be a hint that all is not well with Agamemnon's marriage when he asserts in public that he prefers his concubine Chryseïs to his wife Clytemnestra (1.113-15).

In the *Odyssey*, however, there are several references to the murder of Agamemnon and the revenge of Orestes. Homer systematically contrasts these events with the story of Odysseus and his son Telemachus. Agamemnon returns home incautiously, his wife has taken a lover, and he is killed. Odysseus returns home cautiously, his wife is faithful, and he kills her suitors. Orestes' revenge for his father's murder is held up to Telemachus as a model of what he should do to the suitors (1.293-302; 3.195-209).

The story is basically consistent, although different characters tell it in slightly different ways. Aegisthus wooed Clytemnestra while the other Greeks were at Troy, but she initially resisted. Agamemnon had left her in the care of a bard, but Aegisthus got rid of the bard and took Clytemnestra to his house (3.248-75). He posted a watchman, who after a year reported Agamemnon's return (4.529-35):

> Aegisthus at once laid his foul snare. He chose a score of his strongest townsmen and put them in ambush on one side of the palace; on the other side he ordered a banquet to be prepared. Then he rode forth with chariot and horses to invite Agamemnon to his banquet, but all the while the thoughts of his heart were evil. From shore to city he drove a king who foresaw nothing of his doom; he feasted his guest, then struck him down as a man strikes down an ox at stall.[1]

The ghost of Agamemnon gives his view of what happened when he meets Odysseus in the Underworld (11.412-20):

> Thus I died the most pitiful of deaths, and my comrades too were killed around me mercilessly like white-tusked boars in the house of some rich and powerful man, at a wedding or feast or sumptuous banquet. You have seen in your time many men meet death, in single combat or violent battle, but much more then would compassion have pierced your heart, had you seen how we lay there in the hall by the mixing bowl and the laden tables, while the whole floor seethed with blood.

The usual version in the *Odyssey* is that Agamemnon, along

2. The Story before Sophocles

with his followers, is killed in Aegisthus' house. Aegisthus ruled for seven years, oppressing the people, but in the eighth Orestes returned and killed him (3.304-10).

The main variation in these accounts of the murder of Agamemnon is in the responsibility attributed to Clytemnestra. Aegisthus alone is mentioned as the killer in several passages. Athena reminds Telemachus of Orestes killing 'his father's murderer, that treacherous Aegisthus who slew majestic Agamemnon' (1.299-300; cf. 3.193-8, 305-8; 4.534). Zeus describes how Aegisthus ignored the gods' warnings and was duly punished. He does not even mention Clytemnestra by name, and she figures in his account merely as the seduced wife (1.28-47; cf. 3.265-72). This version of the story stresses the parallel between Aegisthus and the suitors. Clytemnestra sometimes plays a more prominent part in the murder, especially when the speaker is the ghost of Agamemnon himself (11.410, 453; 24.97; 24.200). It is natural that he should focus on the guilt of his treacherous wife, and the change of emphasis is probably due more to the attitude of the speaker than to the influence of a different version of the story. This version also stresses the contrast between Clytemnestra and Odysseus' loyal wife Penelope.

Orestes kills Aegisthus, and gives a funeral feast to the Argives for him and Clytemnestra (3.309-10). Jebb writes: 'The fact that the funeral feast was given "to the Argives" implies that they welcomed Orestes as a deliverer, and also that (whatever had been the manner of his mother's death) they did *not* regard him as resting under any defilement which incapacitated him for religious acts' (p. xi n. 3). Homer certainly emphasizes the positive aspect of Orestes' feat, but it would be mistaken to conclude either that he is implying that the matricide is justified or that he does not know about it at all. He evidently knows about the matricide, but suppresses it. There are two reasons for this. In the first place, it would have disrupted the parallel with the *Odyssey* and undermined Orestes' function as a model for Telemachus. It is common in Greek poetry of all periods for inconvenient elements of exemplary stories to be adapted or omitted. Secondly, Homer tends to suppress or tone down stories about violence or perversity within the family. He thus passes over Alcmaeon's matricide (11.326-7; 15.244-8), Agamemnon's sacrifice of Iphigenia, and the children which Oedipus had with his mother (11.271-4). He probably knew about all these things, but chose to omit them as being unsuitable for epic poetry. If the matricide were really unproblematic, then he would not have needed to take such care to avoid dwelling on it.[2]

The influence of the *Odyssey* on *Electra* is not confined to its treatment of the Orestes myth itself. Orestes resembles Odysseus in returning home in disguise after a long absence, meeting his loved ones, and killing the enemies who have occupied his house. He also resembles Telemachus in being a young man deprived of his father's wealth and position, who is only just of an age to start asserting himself effectively. He has a young travelling companion in Pylades, as does Telemachus in 'Mentor' (actually Athena in disguise) and Pisistratus. The Paedagogus' plausible and fictitious messenger speech in *Electra* recalls the many lying tales which Odysseus tells in the *Odyssey*, cruelly deceiving his loved ones along with his enemies. The *Odyssey* shows that Orestes has good heroic precedent for the use of deception and trickery (*dolos*) in taking revenge (e.g. *Odyssey* 11.454-6; 14.327-30 ~ *Electra* 36-7). Electra resembles Penelope in being the woman who waits at home and weeps, at odds with those who have taken over her house and longing for the return of the man who will release her. Two scenes in particular have Homeric models. The Paedagogus points out to Orestes the landmarks of his homeland at the beginning of *Electra*, just as Athena does to Odysseus when he returns to Ithaca (*Odyssey* 13.344-51). In both cases, the proposal of a stratagem follows immediately. Secondly, the chariot race described by the Paedagogus in the messenger speech (*Electra* 680-763) recalls that in the *Iliad* (23.262-652). In particular, Orestes seems to follow the tactics recommended in the *Iliad* by Nestor (*Electra* 720-2, 743-6 ~ *Iliad* 23.334-41).[3]

2. The Story before Sophocles

Poetry between Homer and Aeschylus

The story also featured in the 'epic cycle', a collection of epic poems composed by various poets in the seventh and sixth centuries. Only a few fragments survive, but we have some knowledge of their contents from summaries by later mythographers. The *Cypria* ('the Cyprian epic', referring to where it was composed) dealt with the preliminaries and earlier stages of the Trojan war. It attributed four daughters to Agamemnon, adding Iphigenia to the three mentioned in the *Iliad*. It described her sacrifice at Aulis as the Greek expedition prepared to sail to Troy:

> Agamemnon killed a deer while hunting and claimed to surpass Artemis herself. The goddess in her wrath stopped them from sailing by sending wild weather. When Calchas told them of the goddess's wrath and said they should sacrifice Iphigeneia to Artemis, they sent for her as if she was to marry Achilles, and set about to sacrifice her.[4]

Artemis rescues Iphigenia in the *Cypria*, and this remained the most popular version of the story. The *Nostoi* ('Returns') dealt with the returns of the Greek heroes from the Trojan war. This work included Orestes' and Pylades' avenging of Agamemnon's murder by Aegisthus and Clytemnestra. The interesting thing here is the first appearance of Pylades, implying that Orestes had been living in Phocis. This in turn suggests that there may have been some connexion with Apollo and his shrine at nearby Delphi.

A fragment of the *Catalogue of Women* (mid-sixth century), attributed in antiquity to Hesiod but not authentic, contains the earliest explicit statement that Orestes killed Clytemnestra (fr. 23a.29-30). Iphigenia is called Iphimede here, and she is saved from sacrifice by Artemis and made immortal. This fragment also has the first surviving reference to Electra, but we learn only that she was 'beautiful as a goddess'. The shadowy poet Xanthus, who may be earlier, said that Electra's original name

23

was Laodice and that she was called Electra because she remained unmarried (*alektros*). This is no doubt an attempt to reconcile the importance of Electra in some versions of the myth with the three daughters of Agamemnon named in the *Iliad*.

Stesichorus (active 600-550 BC) made by far the greatest contribution to the development of the story between Homer and Aeschylus. His *Oresteia* was a lyric poem in two books, of which only meagre fragments survive.[5] He located Agamemnon's kingdom in Sparta, perhaps influenced by contemporary Spartan political claims. The myth in any case left some scope for different views about where Agamemnon and Menelaus lived. There are even passages in Homer which imply, contrary to his usual versions, that Agamemnon lived in Sparta (*Odyssey* 4.514-18) and Menelaus in Mycenae (*Odyssey* 3.249, 256-7, 311). One fragment describes Clytemnestra's dream: 'She dreamed that a snake came, with the top of its head bloodied, and out of it appeared a king of the line of Pleisthenes.' Pleisthenes was Agamemnon's father in some versions. The snake is obviously the dead Agamemnon. The king who grew out of it seems be Orestes, although some scholars argue that it is Agamemnon. Another fragment has Apollo addressing Orestes as he gives him a bow with which to defend himself against the Furies.[6] This implies conflict among the gods about the justice of the matricide. This fragment also attributes to Stesichorus the use of a lock of hair in the recognition of Orestes by Electra. A final detail is that Orestes has a nurse called Laodamia.

The last surviving poetic treatment of the story before Aeschylus is in Pindar's eleventh Pythian ode, which probably dates to 474 BC although there is some evidence for a date of 454 BC (four years after Aeschylus' *Oresteia*). Pindar gives 23 lines to the story (15-37). He locates Agamemnon's palace at Amyclae (near Sparta). He speculates on Clytemnestra's reasons for killing him (22-5):

Was it then the sacrificial slaying of Iphigeneia at Euripos far from her homeland that provoked her to rouse up her

heavy-handed anger? Or did night-time lovemaking lead
her astray by enthralling her to another's bed?[7]

She also kills Cassandra, the concubine whom he had brought
back from Troy (cf. *Odyssey* 11.421-3). Orestes was rescued 'out
from under the powerful hands of Clytemnestra and away from
her grievous treachery' by his nurse Arsinoe, and brought up by
Strophius father of Pylades. He eventually returned to kill
Clytemnestra and Aegisthus with the help of Ares. There is no
mention of Electra. Strophius' kingdom includes Apollo's shrine
at Delphi ('the rich fields of Pylades', 15), but there is no explicit
mention of the god's involvement in the matricide.

The myth in art

Scenes from the story were frequently represented in art.[8] The
earliest surviving example is an Athenian crater (mixing bowl)
by the Ram Jug Painter (*c.* 670 BC). Orestes, holding a sword,
marches Aegisthus forward; Clytemnestra walks before them;
there are traces of a female figure behind Orestes who could
possibly be Electra. The actual killing of Clytemnestra was
never a popular subject, and there is no certain representation
of it before the end of the fifth century. Orestes' killing of
Aegisthus had much greater appeal, since it could be represented as a just act of revenge by a dutiful son. The murder of
Agamemnon is shown on a decorative terracotta plaque from
Gortyn in Crete (630-610 BC). Clytemnestra, aided by Aegisthus, stabs him as he sits on a chair.

Three architectural sculptures from the temple of Hera at
Foce del Sele in South Italy (570-550 BC) depict scenes from the
myth. The first shows Clytemnestra using an axe for the first
time; she is restrained by an unidentified woman. She is not
fully dressed, indicating that she is responding to an emergency. This is not, therefore, the murder of Agamemnon, but an
attempt to defend Aegisthus from Orestes. Another sculpture
shows Orestes stabbing Aegisthus. The third has Orestes trying
to escape from a snaky Fury coiled round him, indicating the

dire consequences of the matricide. These images may have been inspired by Stesichorus' *Oresteia*, but it has been argued that the influence was the other way round or that both drew on a common tradition.

The death of Aegisthus is vividly portrayed on a red-figure vase by the Berlin Painter (*c.* 500 BC), the earliest surviving example of a series of vase-paintings of this theme. The subject may have been inspired by the famous exploit of the Athenian tyrant-slayers Harmodius and Aristogiton (514 BC). The overthrow of tyranny has at various times been perceived as the main subject of *Electra* itself (cf. Chapter 7 n. 15). The figures are identified by inscriptions. Orestes grabs the seated Aegisthus by the hair and stabs him with a sword; Clytemnestra, not fully dressed, intervenes with an axe; she is restrained by Talthybius; Chrysothemis runs off in alarm. Talthybius (Agamemnon's herald) appears in other representations of this scene, and there is evidence for a literary version in which he played a part in the rescue of Orestes at his father's death. The role of the Paedagogus in *Electra* may thus owe something to him.[9] Electra is named as the female figure encouraging Orestes on a red-figure vase by the Triptolemus Painter (*c.* 480 BC), the first certain representation of her in art. A relief from Melos (470-60 BC) shows Electra seated at Agamemnon's tomb, with a female servant behind her; Orestes, Pylades, and a male servant approach. The influence of Aeschylus' *Oresteia* (458 BC) made the recognition of Orestes and Electra the most popular scene from the story in art.

The famous 'Boston Oresteia crater' by the Dokimasia Painter (*c.* 470 BC) shows the murder of Agamemnon on one side and that of Aegisthus on the other. Agamemnon, enveloped in a diaphanous robe but otherwise naked, is stabbed by Aegisthus with a sword; Clytemnestra, carrying an axe, comes up behind Aegisthus to help him. Three other female figures may represent Electra, Chrysothemis, and Cassandra. The other side shows Clytemnestra threatening Orestes with her axe as he kills Aegisthus. Aegisthus, as often, is seated; he holds a lyre as he slumps from his chair; a female figure, who may be Electra, gesticulates to Orestes.

Aeschylus

The main elements of the story were thus well established when Aeschylus (*c.* 525-456 BC) gave it a definitive tragic form in his *Oresteia* (458 BC). The trilogy comprises *Agamemnon, Libation Bearers* (in Greek, *Choephoroe*), and *Eumenides*. The first two plays of the trilogy are set in front of Agamemnon's palace at Argos, which he shared with Menelaus. This is an idiosyncratic response to the question of the location of the palace, about which conflicting versions are apparent as early as the *Odyssey*. 'Argos' in Homer refers to three places: the city of Argos (ruled by Diomedes), the Argolid (Agamemnon's kingdom, with his seat at Mycenae), and the Peloponnese or Greece as a whole. Aeschylus wanted a double kingdom so that Agamemnon is directly the victim of Paris' violation of the house, and Argos is less exclusively identified with either brother than Mycenae or Sparta. The city of Argos was important in 458 BC, and had made an alliance with Athens in 462 to which there is an allusion in *Eumenides* (287-91, 667-73, 762-74). Mycenae (six miles north of Argos) had been far less powerful since the eleventh century, and was destroyed by Argos in the 460s.

Agamemnon deals with the return home of Agamemnon after his victory at Troy. He arrives in triumph about halfway through the play, accompanied by his concubine Cassandra. In the earlier part of the play, the chorus of Argive elders reflected at length on the Greek expedition to Troy, going back to Agamemnon's sacrifice of Iphigenia at Aulis. A messenger brings news of recent events, including the storm on their return voyage in which Menelaus was apparently lost. Clytemnestra, 'a woman whose heart plans like a man' (10), rules in Argos. She deceives Agamemnon on his return, but her murder of him is no mere ambush. She defeats him verbally on stage in the 'carpet scene', ensuring that he enters the house on her terms. Cassandra has a prophetic vision of the palace as a

27

slaughterhouse, but she too goes in to her death. Agamemnon's death cries are heard from within. Clytemnestra has thrown a net over him in his bath, and kills him with (probably) a sword.[10] This version differs from that in Homer, followed by Sophocles, in which Agamemnon is killed at a banquet. Aegisthus is an insignificant figure, who plays no part in the murder and appears only at the end of the play.

Libation Bearers deals with the return and revenge of Orestes, the events of Sophocles' *Electra*. The first half of the play is set by Agamemnon's tomb and the second in front of the palace, although there is no actual scene change and the chorus does not leave the *orchêstra*. Orestes returns as usual with Pylades, but Aeschylus adopts a novel version of the story in which Clytemnestra herself had sent him into exile in Phocis. In all other versions, he is rescued from her by others. He lays a lock of hair on Agamemnon's tomb, and then withdraws as he sees the chorus of slave-women approaching with libations. They are accompanied by Electra, whom he recognizes immediately. Clytemnestra has had a troubling dream, and wishes to propitiate the spirit of Agamemnon. Electra asks the chorus for advice on how to make the offerings, and then appeals to her father's spirit (132-41):

> For we are outcasts now, as it were, sold off by our mother; and she has taken a man in exchange, Aegisthus, her very accomplice in your murder. I am like a slave myself, while Orestes is in exile from his property; and their great and extravagant luxury is the fruit of your labour. That Orestes may come here through some fortune is my prayer to you; and you must hear me, father! Grant me also to be much more chaste than my mother, and my hands to have greater piety.[11]

The recognition is accomplished through the lock of Orestes' hair which Electra finds, then his footprints, and finally a sample of Electra's embroidery which he wears or at least has in his possession. Their ecstatic reunion is cut short by a warning from the chorus, and Orestes describes Apollo's order to avenge the murder. There follows the great *kommos* (306-478), a ritual invocation and lament of Agamemnon in which Orestes, Electra, and the chorus participate. The first half of the play concludes with the revenge-plan. Orestes will kill 'them' by treachery (*dolos*), as they killed Agamemnon. Electra is dispatched into the palace, and plays no further part.

Orestes and Pylades enter disguised as travellers, and tell Clytemnestra that Orestes is dead. She expresses grief (691-9), but this is later reported by Orestes' old nurse Cilissa to have been hypocritical (737-43). Cilissa has been sent to summon Aegisthus, and she is persuaded by the chorus to adapt her message so that he comes without his bodyguard. He is on stage for a mere 17 lines, before going into the palace to be killed. Clytemnestra is summoned, and calls for the 'man-slaying axe' (889) with which she traditionally defends herself in art. She does not get it, and is unarmed for her climactic confrontation with Orestes. He takes her in to be killed, and the chorus sings a celebratory ode. He displays the corpses of Clytemnestra and Aegisthus, confident of the justice of his deed. The mood then changes abruptly. He admits that he is going mad, and departs into exile pursued by the Furies.

Eumenides, the final play of the trilogy, addresses the implications of the matricide, which is treated in the broadest moral, social, political, and theological terms. Orestes, relentlessly pursued by the Furies, seeks refuge in Apollo's temple at Delphi. He is directed to go to Athens, where the matter is finally resolved by trial by jury. He is acquitted on the casting vote of Athena, and she persuades the Furies to bestow blessings on Athens.

Sophocles evidently knew the *Oresteia* well, and *Electra* is full of reminiscences of it. Much of the character of Electra herself can be traced back to her brief appearance in *Libation Bearers*. Her prayer 'to be much more chaste [*sôphrôn*] than my mother' (*Libation Bearers* 140-1, quoted above) becomes in Sophocles a tragic dilemma about how she can really be *sôphrôn* in the circumstances in which she finds herself (*Electra* 307-9, 608-9; cf. Chapter 5). Sophocles' Clytemnestra, too, owes something to the more complex and forceful character in Aeschylus, e.g. her defiant refusal to deny what she has done (*Electra* 525-7 ~ *Agamemnon* 1380-1), and her resentment that Agamemnon sacrificed the fruit of her labour-pains Iphigenia (*Electra* 530-3 ~ *Agamemnon* 1417-18). Electra 'drinks her unmixed blood' (*Electra* 785-6), recalling the vampirical Fury invoked by Aeschylus' Orestes (*Libation Bearers* 577-8, where the reference to neat wine is more explicit). Her death-cries echo those of the husband whom she killed (*Electra* 1415-16 ~ *Agamemnon* 1343-5). Orestes' ornate description of the urn as 'a moulded thing with sides of bronze' (*Electra* 54) alludes to the Aeschylean Orestes' phrase 'the sides of a bronze urn' (*Libation Bearers* 686), and the significance of the urn itself can only be appreciated with reference to Aeschylus (see Chapter 4). Another striking expression is the word *aglaïsma* ('ornament', literally 'that which gives joy'), used by both Chrysothemis (*Electra* 908) and Electra (*Libation Bearers* 193) for the lock of Orestes' hair which they have discovered. Aegisthus, like Aeschylus' Clytemnestra, immediately understands Orestes' riddle that the dead are killing the living (*Electra* 1477-80 ~ *Libation Bearers* 886-7). This list could be considerably extended, and the reminiscences are even more striking in the original Greek. The point is not that Sophocles follows Aeschylus in any literal or slavish way, but that *Electra* has a close intertextual relationship with the *Oresteia* and can only be understood with reference to it.

Sophocles' audience had every opportunity to be familiar with Aeschylus' plays. The Athenians had passed a decree after his death which authorized their revival at the dramatic festivals. Alan Sommerstein has suggested that they had even become school texts by the end of the fifth century. There is ample evidence elsewhere for Aeschylus' influence on his successors. Martin Cropp thus comments on Euripides' *Electra*: 'Aeschylus' *Oresteia* was in many ways definitive, and its presence in Euripides' play is pervasive.' Aeschylus' *Seven Against Thebes* (467 BC) is similarly pervasive in Euripides' *Phoenician Women* (409 BC). Aeschylus' impact was not confined to tragedy.

2. The Story before Sophocles

K.J. Dover remarks on 'the considerable extent of Aeschylean reminiscences, allusions, and parody in Old Comedy'. This is especially notable in Aristophanes' *Frogs* (405 BC), where Aeschylus is a major character and there is an elaborate discussion of the first three lines of *Libation Bearers* (*Frogs* 1124-69).[12]

Euripides

Euripides' *Electra* is now generally dated to the period 422-417 BC, rather than to 413, as was once believed.[13] This makes it somewhat more likely that it preceded Sophocles' *Electra*, although certainty is impossible. There is nothing in Sophocles' *Electra* that benefits from being explained as a response to Euripides' *Electra*, but the two plays were certainly close in date and there is much to be gained from a comparison.

Euripides departs radically from tradition by setting the play away from the palace, in the countryside of the Argolid near the border. Electra has been married off to a poor farmer in order to ensure that she does not have noble sons who might have threatened Clytemnestra and Aegisthus. Euripides presents the story in a 'realistic' mode, emphasizing its more mundane and even squalid aspects. Different views have been expressed about the implications of this for his presentation of the characters and the murders. Aegisthus regains something of the significance which he had lost in Aeschylus, even though he only appears on stage as a corpse. He shared in the murder of Agamemnon, and rules the land. Clytemnestra is correspondingly somewhat gentler and less dominant. Orestes was rescued by Agamemnon's Paedagogus from being killed by Aegisthus, and brought up in Phocis in the usual way.

The novel setting has implications for Euripides' management of the plot. Clytemnestra and Aegisthus must be brought out into the country where the action takes place. The deceptive report of Orestes' death is omitted, and Clytemnestra is enticed to Electra's cottage with the lie that she has given birth. Orestes recognizes Electra almost at once, but delays identifying himself. The Paedagogus brings news of the offerings at

Agamemnon's tomb, but Electra refuses to believe that Orestes was responsible for them. Aegisthus has come out into the country to sacrifice to the Nymphs, and his death is described in a messenger speech. Orestes hesitates before killing Clytemnestra, as in Aeschylus, but Electra overcomes his doubts. She not only exhorts him to strike, as in Sophocles, but plays an active part in the murder. The mood of the end of the play is grim, emphasizing the horror of matricide and the dispersal of the family.

Orestes is a leading figure in three other plays by Euripides: *Andromache* (*c.* 425 BC), *Iphigenia among the Taurians* (*c.* 414 BC), and *Orestes* (408 BC). In *Andromache*, he re-enacts in a new context his definitive story-pattern of surreptitious arrival, reunion with a female relative, and murder with the aid of Apollo. In *Iphigenia among the Taurians*, he stops short of murder but the pattern is otherwise similar. *Orestes* is a kind of sequel to *Electra*, in which the fate of Orestes and Electra is treated in secular and political terms. Orestes is portrayed as a desperado and terrorist, although there is, as always in tragedy, some sympathy for his predicament. He is generally known as 'the mother-killer' (e.g. *Andromache* 999, *Orestes* 479), and his manic behaviour seems to show that one who has committed such a crime will henceforth stop at nothing. It should be stressed that Orestes only takes on this character after the matricide, which is not represented in Euripides' *Electra* as an act of lunacy. He is attacked by the Furies in both *Iphigenia among the Taurians* and *Orestes*, and their pursuit of him is mentioned in *Andromache* (978). The deranged Orestes was evidently such a popular figure on the tragic stage that new opportunities had to be found for him to display his characteristic pattern of behaviour.

It is worth observing in this context that 'Orestes' was the nickname of a notorious Athenian mugger, who allegedly attacked people by night and stole their cloaks. He is mentioned by Aristophanes at *Acharnians* 1167-8 (425 BC) and *Birds* 712, 1490-3 (414 BC). Orestes has become a byword for a violent madman.

The Action of the Play

The action of a Greek tragedy is usually continuous, but all tragedies are divided into clearly defined sections. The main structural principle is the alternation of speech and song. In particular, every tragedy contains a number of odes, or songs, by the chorus. These odes punctuate the action. Aristotle offered the most influential discussion of the structure of a Greek tragedy in *Poetics*, ch. 12 (1452b). He defined the *prologos* as the part of a tragedy before the entrance of the chorus, an *epeisodion* as what happens between two choral odes, and the *exodos* as the section after the last choral ode. The first choral ode is termed the *parodos*, and every choral ode thereafter is termed a *stasimon*. Aristotle's analysis is not entirely satisfactory, since he tends to overlook that a tragedy can be articulated in other ways than by choral odes, but his terminology is in common use and is mentioned in parentheses in the subheadings below.

Oliver Taplin has given the best account of the structure of a Greek tragedy in *The Stagecraft of Aeschylus*, pp. 49-60. Taplin's advance was to look not only at the alternation of speech and song but also at the exits and entrances of actors. He pointed out that there are regularly exits immediately before choral odes and entrances immediately after them. The strongest structural divisions in a tragedy combine a choral ode with a rearrangement of the actors. Act divisions are typically marked by the following sequence: exit actor(s) – choral ode – enter new actor(s). There are many variations on this basic pattern. In particular, Taplin was able to show that the lyric element in these structural divisions does not have to be a full-scale choral ode. It can be a short song by the chorus or a lyric dialogue between the chorus and one or more actors. Such lyrics are 'act-dividing' because they are accompanied by substantial rearrangement of the actors. The lyric dialogue between Electra and the chorus at *Electra* 823-70 divides two acts because it is preceded (at 803) by the exits of Clytemnestra and the Paedagogus and followed immediately by the entrance of Chrysothemis. This structural division is as emphatic as any involving a choral ode. Aristotle's analysis, by contrast, would include this lyric in one huge *epeisodion* stretching from 516 to 1057.

Electra can, on these principles, be divided into eleven sections:

(1)	First act (*prologos*)	41-120
(2)	Entry of the chorus (*parodos*)	121-250
(3)	Second act (first *epeisodion*)	251-471
(4)	First choral ode (first *stasimon*)	472-515
(5)	Third act (second *epeisodion*, part 1)	516-822
(6)	Lyric dialogue	823-70
(7)	Fourth act (second *epeisodion*, part 2)	871-1057
(8)	Second choral ode (second *stasimon*)	1058-97
(9)	Fifth act (third *epeisodion*)	1098-383
(10)	Third choral ode (third *stasimon*)	1384-97
(11)	Sixth act (*exodos*)	1398-1510

Background

The scene is set in Mycenae, in front of the palace of the Pelopidae (descendants of Pelops). Agamemnon, grandson of Pelops and king of Mycenae, was murdered on his return from the Trojan War by his wife Clytemnestra and her lover Aegisthus, also a grandson of Pelops. Orestes, only son of Agamemnon and Clytemnestra, was a child at the time of his father's death. He was smuggled away from Mycenae by his older sister Electra, and brought up by his father's ally Strophius, king of Crisa in Phocis. This was near Delphi, the oracular shrine of the god Apollo. Pylades, the son of Strophius, is Orestes' inseparable friend. Electra remained in the palace at Mycenae, loyal to her father's memory and implacably hostile to Clytemnestra and Aegisthus. She is unmarried, and treated as little more than a slave. Another sister, Chrysothemis, has reconciled herself to the new régime and in consequence enjoys a more comfortable existence. This state of affairs has continued for many years, but Orestes is now old enough to return from exile and claim his father's kingdom.

First act (*prologos*) 1-120

Three men enter by an *eisodos*, one of the two side-entrances to the left and right of the stage. It is dawn, and no one else is yet about. Two of the men are young noblemen, while the third is an elderly slave. One of the young men is Orestes, and his entrance is a highly significant dramatic event. It is the long-awaited return of the exile and arrival of the avenger. Electra has been sustained for years by the hope that he will one day return (171-2, 303-4, 317-23), while Clytemnestra has lived in terror of him (293-8, 778-82). Now he has come. A further point is that he has returned with only two companions to help him. Unlike Polynices in the Theban myth, he has not brought an army which might have threatened the whole city.

The other young man is Pylades. His role in the play is as Orestes' faithful friend. Friendship was a prominent topic in Greek ethics, and Pylades is the outstanding example in myth of the ideal friend.[1] He shows his qualities especially by remaining loyal to Orestes in his greatest need. Greek has a special grammatical form, the dual, which is used for pairs (e.g. eyes, hands). The dual is used frequently in *Electra* of Orestes and Pylades (21, 75, 1297, 1367, 1376, 1401), emphasizing the close connexion of the two men. A dramatic convention which Sophocles exploits is that Pylades, as the less important member of an established pair, never speaks. This seems to have been especially common with pairs of brothers. Castor is thus the only one of the Dioscuri to speak at the end of Euripides' *Electra* and *Helen*, although his brother Polydeuces (= Pollux) is also present. Pylades also remains silent throughout Euripides'

Electra, and it is partly this convention which makes the three lines which he does speak in Aeschylus' *Libation Bearers* (900-2) so effective. The convenience of the convention lay in making economical use of the three speaking actors to which tragedians were limited. Orestes only addresses Pylades once (1372-5), but his constant presence should not be forgotten when reading the play.

The older man in the group is Orestes' paedagogus, whose title is rendered in a variety of ways by translators (e.g. 'tutor', 'old man'). A 'paedagogus' was a trusted slave who looked after the education of a boy in his earlier years, escorted him when he went out, and even accompanied him to school. The paedagogus of Medea's two sons appears with them at the beginning of Euripides' *Medea* (46-95), and Agamemnon's old paedagogus plays a crucial part in Euripides' *Electra*. A paedagogus could act as a confidential servant long after his tutoring days were over. Themistocles employed his sons' paedagogus Sicinnus to convey his momentous message to the Persians before the battle of Salamis (Herodotus 8.75). In Euripides' *Ion*, the Athenian princess Creusa is accompanied on her visit to Delphi by the former paedagogus of her father Erechtheus, and she treats him as a surrogate father (Euripides, *Ion* 725-34; cf. *Electra* 1361). This individual shows how a paedagogus can be devoted to what he sees as the interests of the family when they are threatened by an outsider who marries into it (Euripides, *Ion* 808-29). The Paedagogus in *Electra* has an absolute loyalty to Agamemnon which is not diluted by any blood tie to Clytemnestra.

Sophocles typically begins his plays with dialogue, in contrast to the expository monologues favoured by Euripides. The Paedagogus describes to Orestes the landscape which he has been longing to see again (see Chapter 4 for discussion of this passage). He then gets rapidly to the point, reminding him that he brought him up to avenge his father and urging him to formulate a plan of action. He repeatedly presses upon Orestes the urgency of action (15-22, 82-5, 1326-38, 1344-5, 1364-71). This need for urgency is associated with the word *kairos* (22, 31,

39, 75-6, 1259, 1292, 1368), which refers to what is appropriate, opportune, or effective, and often carries an implication of the avoidance of digression or delay.

Orestes reveals that Apollo's oracle has commanded 'that alone, and by stealth, without the aid of an army, I should secretly accomplish the slaughter by my own righteous hand' (36-7). The key word here is *dolos* ('stealth', 'cunning', 'treachery'). In Aeschylus, Apollo ordered Orestes to use the same *dolos* to kill Clytemnestra and Aegisthus that they had used to kill Agamemnon (*Libation Bearers* 555-9). So too in Sophocles, Agamemnon was killed by *dolos* (124, 197, 279) and his murderers must perish in the same way (1227-9, 1391-7). Orestes makes a solemn prayer to be restored to his homeland, house, and possessions, strongly emphasizing the justice of his mission. He concludes his opening speech by saying that *kairos* 'is in supreme charge of every human action' (75-6). Kells remarks that Orestes' language suggests 'a carefully-planned military operation' (p. 86), and he is in general characterized by a certain unreflective efficiency.

The three men are about to leave the stage when they hear an anguished cry from inside the palace. Orestes rightly suspects that the cry was uttered by Electra, but the Paedagogus insists that he proceed immediately to Agamemnon's grave. Orestes and Pylades thus exit by one *eisodos*, which will henceforth be identified as the way to Agamemnon's grave, while the Paedagogus exits by the other. This staging differs strikingly from other versions. Aeschylus (*Libation Bearers* 16-21) and Euripides (*Electra* 107-11) both have Orestes and Pylades remain on stage in hiding in order to observe Electra. They thus meet soon afterwards, and recognition follows. Sophocles alludes to this possibility, but immediately rejects it. The effect would have been quite different if Orestes and Pylades had departed – as they easily could have done – without being aware of Electra at all.

There is briefly a vacant stage before Electra enters from the palace and sings a lament (86-120). There is a marked contrast with the tone of the earlier part of the act. Earlier we saw three men, two of them evidently noblemen, arriving from outside, speaking iambic trimeters (the usual metre of the spoken parts of tragedy), and determined on action. Now we see a single woman, squalidly dressed (190-1, 451-2), emerging from the palace, singing a lament, and depending on outside help to achieve vengeance. The first act has set out the terms of the action, which will be developed in what follows.

Entry of the chorus (*parodos*) 121-250

The chorus enters, a group of fifteen women of Mycenae. Their age and marital status are left unclear. They address Electra as 'child' (121, 154, 174) and advise her 'like a mother' (234), but this terminology derives from their role as sympathetic advisers and need not indicate their age. They may be referred to as 'women' (e.g. 254), rather than as 'maidens', but the former term can include the latter. What is certain is that they are friends of Electra (134, 226, 307) and hostile to Clytemnestra and Aegisthus (124-8). They are 'noble' (129), although this may only refer to their character, and 'citizen women' (1227). See Chapter 4 for further discussion of the identity and role of the chorus.

Sophocles brings on the chorus in *Electra* in a way that was especially favoured by Euripides. Its appearance is preceded by an actor's monody (i.e. solo song), and its own initial contribution (*parodos*) is in the form of a lyric dialogue with that actor (cf. *Andromache, Trojan Women*). The effect of this is to subordinate the chorus to the actor in dramatic impact, and to smooth over the considerable structural disjunction that can be caused by the entry of the chorus. Contrast Sophocles' *Antigone*, where the stage is cleared before the arrival of the chorus, and the *parodos* consists of a song by the chorus alone. In *Antigone* there is thus a sharp, and highly effective, break between the first act and the *parodos*. The *parodos* of Sophocles' *Electra* has the same basic form as that of Euripides' *Electra*, although there is a difference of emphasis. Euripides has a 55-line monody and a 46-line lyric dialogue between Electra and

38

the chorus, while Sophocles has a 35-line monody and a 130-line lyric dialogue with the chorus. Sophocles thus gives more space to the lyric dialogue, stressing the unwavering resistance of his heroine.

Second act (first *epeisodion*) 251-471

The beginning of this act violates Taplin's structural principles, sketched above. It is normal for there to be an entry after a choral ode or other act-dividing lyric, and this is the case everywhere else in *Electra*. Entries directly after the *parodos* make an especially strong dramatic impact (e.g. in Sophocles' *Antigone* and Euripides' *Medea*). There is no entry here, and Electra continues her dialogue with the chorus. This is a highly purposeful piece of dramaturgy by Sophocles. Electra is the main character in the play, and it would detract from this pre-eminence for anyone else to enter at such a structurally significant moment. Sophocles also, as we saw, subordinated the arrival of the chorus to his heroine at the beginning of the *parodos*. He thus creates a continuous structure overlapping the act division, in which Electra explains her behaviour in dialogue with the chorus (86-323). A degree of structural fluidity is a feature of Sophocles' style, especially in his later plays, and it serves here to highlight Electra's isolation and despair.

Electra begins this act by making a long speech of self-justification and complaint (254-309), which recapitulates many of the points she made in the preceding lyric dialogue: her behaviour may be shameful and excessive, but she is compelled to act as she does (254-7, 307-9 ~ 221-5); the current state of affairs would be intolerable to any right-thinking person (257-60 ~ 226-32, 236-50); she is treated like a slave in her father's house (262-5 ~ 185-92); she continually laments Agamemnon, brooding on the terrible day when he was killed (282-6 ~ 132-3, 145-52, 201-8); she waits for Orestes, but he does not come (303-6 ~ 164-72). The speech gives more precise details about Aegisthus' usurpation of her father's place and about the perverted monthly festival with which her mother celebrates his death (266-81). Electra also gives a vivid account, enlivened by directly quoted speech, of the rebukes which she has to endure from Clytemnestra and Aegisthus (287-302). One of these rebukes, that Electra is not the only person to have lost her father, has also been voiced by the chorus (289-90 ~ 153-4). She stresses both what she has to listen to (288, 293, 295, 299) and what she has to look upon (258, 260, 267, 268, 271, 282).

Sophocles exploits here a tragic convention whereby, as A.M. Dale put it, 'a situation is realized first in its lyric, then in its iambic aspect – that is to say, first emotionally, then in its reasoned form'.[2] This structure also occurs at the corresponding point of Euripides' *Electra* (300-38). John Gould argues that 'the stylization of dramatic form itself shapes and refracts the presentation of human character' (pp. 90-1), so that the characters are 'fragmented and discontinuous' and impossible to interpret merely in terms of 'human intelligibility'. On the other hand, tragedians usually make the transition from lyrics to iambics intelligible to some extent in psychological terms, and at least gesture towards continuity of character from one section to the other. Electra thus begins her speech by saying to the chorus 'I am ashamed, women, if you think that I grieve too much with my many laments; but forgive me, since a hard compulsion forces me to do this' (254-7). She is referring to what she does every day (for *thrênos*, 'lament', cf. 94, 104, 232), but her words can also be taken as a justification of her contribution to the immediately preceding lyrics.

Electra's speech is followed by a brief conversation with the chorus about the whereabouts of Aegisthus and Orestes (310-23). She stresses that Aegisthus is away in the country, and that she would not have had the freedom to come outside if he had been present in the palace. Aegisthus' absence, and the possibility of his return, are mentioned repeatedly during the play (386, 517, 627, 1308, 1368-9, 1402-3). He does not in the event return until near the end (1442). The absence of a male authority figure leaves room for the women to act more freely, as in Euripides' *Hippolytus*, *Andromache*, and *Bacchae*. The other crucial male figure in the story is Orestes, and Electra goes on to express frustration about his failure to return. The absence of these two men, to which this brief conversation draws attention, means that the atmosphere of most of the play is intensely female, with the Paedagogus the only male character to appear between lines 86 and 1098.

A new character now enters from the palace. This is Electra's sister Chrysothemis, whom the chorus has already mentioned as an example of bearing grief more calmly (158). She is much better dressed than her sister (359-62), and the contrast with Electra's squalid clothes makes visible the contrast between the lives which they have chosen. Euripides also relished such contrasts in female dress, which occur in his *Andromache*, *Electra*, *Trojan Women*, and *Orestes*. Chrysothemis does not appear in Aeschylus or Euripides, and Sophocles has developed her role to provide a foil to Electra. All his plays have a character of this type, who tries to persuade the hero(ine) to behave in a less extreme fashion. Ismene (in *Antigone*) is the closest parallel. Chrysothemis says that she is grieved by what is happening and agrees that Electra is right to object to it, but sees nothing to be gained from a futile struggle against necessity. She expresses her attitude in the paradox 'if I am to live in freedom, I must obey the authorities in everything' (339-40). Electra pours out her contempt for this collaboration, and argues that she can at least succeed in honouring her father and vexing her mother. Chrysothemis then announces that if Electra does not cease from her lamentations she will be confined in a sunless dungeon outside the land (380-2). Electra is undeterred even by this appalling threat, and her resistance to her sister's pleas erupts in a passage of stichomythia (385-414). This is a conventional form of dialogue, common in tragedy, whereby each speaker utters one line in turn. It combines rapidity with formal strictness, and is used by Sophocles to heighten tension and excitement at the climax of a scene (cf. 1023-1049, 1176-1219).

Chrysothemis is distinguished by a second visible feature, apart from her clothing, and that is the grave-offerings which she is carrying in her hands. She may be accompanied by one or more attendants to help her with this task, but it is clear that she is carrying at least some of the items herself (326, 431). The chorus remarked on them when she entered, but Sophocles keeps the audience in suspense about their purpose during her dispute with Electra. The offerings will include vessels containing such soothing liquids as milk, honey, wine, and water, as well as flowers to be placed on the grave (cf. Orestes' offerings, 893-6). Sophocles alludes to the beginning of Aeschylus' *Libation Bearers*, where Orestes and Pylades observe Electra and the eponymous chorus bringing offerings to the grave of Agamemnon. The differences are also striking. The offerings are now carried by Chrysothemis, and Orestes is not present to observe them. Sophocles elegantly finds Chrysothemis a role in the plot as well as using her as a foil to Electra.

Chrysothemis explains that Clytemnestra has sent her with the offerings as the result of a dream. 'It is said that she saw our father, restored to the sunlight and living with her once more; then he took the sceptre which he used to carry, and which is now carried by Aegisthus, and planted it by the hearth; and from it a fruitful bough grew up, which overshadowed the whole land of Mycenae' (417-23). This dream is less violent than that described in Aeschylus' *Libation Bearers* (527-33), where Clytemnestra dreamed that she had given birth to a snake, which then drew blood along with milk when she suckled it.

Aeschylus' Electra both carried the offerings and expressed doubts about her role as the agent of Clytemnestra. Sophocles divides Aeschylus' Electra into two, with Chrysothemis conveying the offerings and Electra expressing objections. Aeschylus' Electra decides, after discussion with the chorus, to subvert the intention of Clytemnestra's offerings by accompanying them with a prayer for vengeance (*Libation Bearers* 84-151). Sophocles' Electra persuades Chrysothemis to dispose of Clytemnestra's offerings altogether, and replace them with different ones. These new offerings will be a lock of each sister's hair, together with Electra's girdle. The offering of hair to the dead is often mentioned in Greek literature, going back to Achilles' offering to Patroclus in Homer's *Iliad* (23.140-53). The most famous such gesture was Orestes' offering to Agamemnon, which is prominent in all three tragedians' treatment of the myth. Electra establishes a link with her father which is parallel to, but independent of, that of Orestes. She actually cuts the lock on stage, as Teucer does at Sophocles, *Ajax* 1179 and Orestes may have done at the beginning of Aeschylus' *Libation Bearers*. There are historical parallels for offering garments at tombs (e.g. Thucydides 3.58.4), and the point here is that Electra's girdle is both a very humble item and the only spare piece of clothing that she possesses. Chrysothemis then exits by the same *eisodos* as was previously used by Orestes and Pylades. Electra remains on stage during the ensuing choral ode.

First choral ode (first *stasimon*) 472-515

The lyric (i.e. sung) parts of tragedy are usually arranged in pairs of stanzas ('strophic pairs'), comprising a *strophê* and an *antistrophê*. The metrical structure of the two stanzas, and doubtless also the choreography, are identical. This short choral ode comprises one strophic pair and an epode (i.e. a single stanza with a different metrical structure). In the *strophê*, the chorus reassures Electra that Justice sent the dream and will soon come to pursue the murderers. Agamemnon is not forgetful, and even the axe which killed him bears a grudge against those who used it. In the *antistrophê*, the chorus expresses confidence that the unwearying Fury is about to ambush the murderers like a mighty army. If Clytemnestra's dream is not fulfilled, then no dream or oracle could ever again be taken as a portent. 'Electra herself has acquired assurance from the dream ..., but it is left to the chorus to give form to what is in her mind and to affirm the justice of her hopes for vengeance' (Burton, p. 198).

The epode takes us back to the chariot race of Pelops. Sophocles treats this famous story in the most allusive terms. Pelops won his bride Hippodamia by defeating her father Oenomaus in a chariot race. He succeeded by bribing his rival's charioteer Myrtilus to sabotage his master's chariot, so that he was killed in a crash during the race. The two men soon quarrelled, and Pelops killed Myrtilus by hurling him into the sea from the golden chariot with winged horses which he had been given by the sea-god Poseidon. Myrtilus cursed him, and this curse is treated here as the origin of the troubles of his house. Sophocles uses the same word *aikeia* ('violence', 'outrage') to describe the deaths of both Agamemnon (487; cf. 102, 206) and Myrtilus (511). This is also the final word of the ode, as the chorus remarks that *aikeia* has not left the house since the death of Myrtilus (515). The *strophê* and *antistrophê* look forward to a just act of retribution, while the epode sees the history of the family as an unending sequence of cruelty, deception, and violence.

Third act (second *epeisodion*, part 1) 516-822

Clytemnestra enters from the palace, the third major female character in the play to do so. She is accompanied by a female slave carrying offerings of various fruits, whose recipient and purpose will only later become clear. The first part of the act (down to line 633) consists of a formal debate, or agon, between Clytemnestra and Electra. The Greek word *'agôn'* is applied to a variety of verbal and other contests, including trials in the lawcourts, and the word is used in English as a technical term for a particular kind of scene in tragedy. The standard form of such scenes is that two characters make opposing set speeches, and then engage in angry dialogue in a less formal style. Sometimes, although not in *Electra*, there is a judgement speech by a third party. Such agon scenes are especially common in Euripides, who has a liking for distinct formal units in his plays. These scenes are not merely informal quarrels, but have a standard form which would have aroused corresponding expectations in the audience. In particular, it is normal for speakers to demonstrate considerable rhetorical expertise and to express themselves in a manner which may seem to us more appropriate to a public forum than to a domestic dispute. Fifth-century Athenian male citizens had many opportunities to listen to – and indeed to make – public speeches in forensic and political contexts, and were notorious connoisseurs of public speaking. The agon form is an aspect of this mode of conducting moral, legal, and political disputes. It is just one example of the paradoxical role of women in tragedy that they can adopt a formal and public mode of speaking which they would have had no opportunity to practise in real life.

It is normal in these agon scenes for the plaintiff to speak first, as in the lawcourts.[3] Clytemnestra is the defendant here, but she speaks first because she has been criticized by Electra so often in the past that a further prosecution speech would be superfluous. Sophocles conveys a powerful sense that this is only the latest in an interminable series of such confrontations, as Clytemnestra keeps referring to what Electra 'often' or 'always' says about her. Electra herself earlier quoted examples of Clytemnestra's contributions to these scenes (287-98). Clytemnestra defends herself vigorously, and her defiance recalls her attitude at the end of Aeschylus' *Agamemnon* (1380). In Euripides' *Electra*, by contrast, she expresses regret for the murder (1105-10). Electra makes a formal request for permission to speak before beginning her reply. Clytemnestra grants it, but later changes her mind and threatens Electra with punishment for her insolence (626-9). The point of this is partly to smooth over the improbability of the tyrannical Clytemnestra allowing herself to be abused at length by her daughter (cf. Euripides, *Electra* 1049-59). Secondly, this exchange marks explicitly that we are watching an agon, so that we can now expect to hear a substantial speech from Electra. Such formal clarity is more typical of Euripides than of Sophocles. Electra's speech will be discussed in Chapter 5.

The effect of an agon is always to make the hostility worse, and the two main speeches are usually followed by angry dialogue. This is the case here, as Clytemnestra accuses Electra of shamelessness and she in turn retorts that her behaviour, unseemly as it may be, is prompted by the intolerable situation in which she has been placed. Stichomythia is common in this section of an agon. This dialogue includes a brief passage of distichomythia, or dialogue in which each character speaks two lines. In Euripides, the end of an agon is almost always marked by the exit of one or both of the participants. Hostility has generally reached such a pitch that they cannot remain on stage together. It is a significant piece of stagecraft here that Electra and Clytemnestra both remain on stage after the conclusion of the agon (633). Sophocles conveys that the two women cannot escape from each other, however great their mutual hatred.

Clytemnestra now reveals that she has come out of the palace with offerings in order to pray to Apollo. By the street door of many Athenian houses stood an image of Apollo Agyieus ('god of the streets') in the form of a pointed stone pillar, as well perhaps as an altar. There are several references to this feature in Athenian drama, and the rather casual tone of some of them suggests that it was routinely present on the stage. Clytemnestra prays to Apollo Agyieus here both because he is conveniently close, and because in this role he 'stands before' the house as its protector (637). She is disturbed by her dream, and prays that if it means good for her it should be fulfilled, and that if it means harm it should recoil upon her enemies. This is a conventional response to a troubling dream, and is advised by the chorus of elders to the Persian queen Atossa in Aeschylus' *Persians* (215-25). She then prays that no enemies be permitted to eject her from her present prosperity by stealth, and that she continue to rule in the company of those who are well-disposed towards her. Apollo has actually commanded Orestes to kill her by stealth (37), so her prayer is doomed to disappointment. The prayers of Orestes (67-72) and Electra (1376-83) will, by contrast, be fulfilled. Clytemnestra expresses her prayer in veiled language because of the hostile presence of Electra, and concludes by expressing confidence that Apollo will understand what she has not said aloud. What she does not do explicitly is to describe the contents of the dream or to identify her friends and enemies by name.

The Paedagogus now enters by an *eisodos*, presumably the same one by which he departed earlier. Sophocles does not enter into the question of what he has been doing in the meantime, or

46

why he chooses this particular moment to appear, since minor characters have little or no offstage existence. Orestes' instructions (38-50) have prepared for his appearance at some point, but his entrance at this particular moment is surprising and dramatic. The effect is of events occurring unpredictably and as if by coincidence, while also having a hidden meaning. It has often been observed that the Paedagogus arrives as if in answer to Clytemnestra's prayer, although he is in fact executing a plot which will have an effect opposite to that for which she hoped. Jocasta's prayer at *Oedipus the King* 911-23 is similarly followed by an entrance which seems initially to fulfil it, while in reality precipitating the tragic dénouement.

The Paedagogus had earlier been instructed to report that Orestes had been killed in a chariot crash at the Pythian games at Delphi (47-50), and he chooses to elaborate this information in an 84-line speech. The significance of this 'messenger' speech will be discussed in Chapter 4. This is the first scene in the play to have three speaking actors on stage at once. Sophocles highlights the contrast between Electra's grief-stricken reaction to the news of Orestes' death and Clytemnestra's eagerness to hear more. After the Paedagogus' speech, Clytemnestra's response is ambiguous: 'O Zeus, what shall I call this news? Am I to call it fortunate, or terrible but beneficial? It is a painful thing, if I save my life by my own troubles' (766-8). She goes on to admit that she is relieved that she need no longer fear Orestes' threats, but different views have been expressed about the genuineness of her sorrow. She seems almost to regard Electra as the greater menace, and after a brief exchange of taunts with her she escorts the Paedagogus into the palace. Electra, in despair, determines no longer to live inside as a slave with the murderers of her father, but to waste away her life at the door.

Lyric dialogue 823-70

The *parodos* took the form of a lyric dialogue, and here we have the somewhat rarer phenomenon of an act-dividing lyric dialogue later in a play. Its act-dividing status is made clear by the exits of Clytemnestra and the Paedagogus shortly before it and the entry of Chrysothemis immediately after it. Sophocles avoids marking the act division with a full-scale choral ode. This reflects some reduction in the importance of the chorus in the later fifth century, and has the dramatic purpose of keeping the focus on Electra in her despair. It is not clear whether the chorus' contributions were sung by the whole chorus or by the leader alone. Some of their interjections are so brief that it is difficult to imagine them being sung by all fifteen chorus members.

This lyric dialogue has two strophic pairs, and resembles the *parodos* in that Electra resists sympathetic attempts at consolation by the chorus. The structure is somewhat different, in that there is now much more rapid interchange between them. The emotional intensity is greater. In the fourteen lines of the first *strophê*, for example, there are seven changes of singer. Some of Electra's contributions are reduced to inarticulate (and untranslatable) outbursts of grief: 'eh eh, aiai!', 'pheu!', 'eh eh, io!'. Sophocles even shares individual lines between actor and chorus, the earliest example of this in his extant plays, and evidence of an increasingly flexible approach to dramatic structure.

Electra will accept no hint from the chorus that Orestes may yet be alive. For her, he has 'manifestly' (832) gone to Hades. The chorus cites the example of Amphiaraus, who was killed by the treachery of his wife, but was avenged by his son Alcmaeon and is now mighty in the underworld. Electra retorts that she no longer has an avenger. The chorus attempts to console her, but Orestes' death has deprived her of all hope (860-70, trans. Jebb, slightly adapted):

CHORUS: For all men it is appointed to die.
ELECTRA: What, to die as that ill-starred one died, amid the tramp of racing steeds, entangled in the reins that dragged him?
CHORUS: Cruel was his doom, beyond thought!

ELECTRA: Yes, surely; when in foreign soil, without ministry of my hands –
CHORUS: Alas!
ELECTRA: – he is buried, ungraced by me with burial or with tears.

Fourth act (second *epeisodion*, part 2) 871-1057

Chrysothemis enters by the *eisodos* which will by now be associated with the way to Agamemnon's grave. She is in a state of high excitement, since she has found Orestes' offerings on the grave and is convinced that he has returned. There could not be a greater contrast with Electra's state of mind. Violent contrasts of mood are a feature of Sophocles' plays, but this one is unusual. His normal technique is to have an outburst of deluded euphoria by the chorus immediately before the catastrophe. This happens in four of his seven surviving plays, including *Antigone* (1115-54) and *Oedipus the King* (1086-1109). The difference here is that Chrysothemis' euphoria is not deluded, and it is Electra's despair that is unfounded.

Sophocles' use of Chrysothemis in this scene is a good example of his style as a playwright. Aeschylus' *Libation Bearers* takes place at the tomb of Agamemnon, so that the discovery by Electra of the evidence for Orestes' visit takes place on stage. In Sophocles' and Euripides' treatments of the story, the tomb is off stage and we must hear of Orestes' offerings at second hand. Euripides uses Agamemnon's old paedagogus, who has made a detour past the tomb on his way to Electra's house, to describe them. Sophocles prefers a more economical solution. Chrysothemis already has an integral role in the play as the foil character to Electra, and her dialogue with Electra develops this. We have also seen her go off to Agamemnon's tomb for a stated purpose, and have thus been expecting her return. She appears with her joyful news at exactly the moment of Electra's greatest despair, with a carefully calculated effect on the emotional sequence of the play. The uncanny timing of her arrival is on one level a matter of dramatic economy, but may also be taken to suggest a pattern to events beyond the merely coincidental.

Oedipus the King is famous for Sophocles' exploration of the language of investigation and deduction, a subject of particular interest in late fifth-century Athens. There is a similarly systematic treatment of the topic here. Chrysothemis says that Orestes is present 'as manifestly as you see me' (878), but Electra can only ask from whom she heard this 'story' in which she places such excessive trust (883-4). Chrysothemis insists 'I believe this story on my own authority, not another's, having seen clear evidence' (885-6). She then begins her account by insisting that she will tell everything that she saw, and uses seven more verbs of seeing in the first fifteen lines of her speech. In the second half of her speech, she spells out her deduction from this visual evidence, that no one other than Orestes could have left these offerings at the tomb. She uses the semi-technical term *tekmêrion* ('proof', 904), which appears in a forensic context as early as Aeschylus' *Eumenides* (485, 662).[4] The result of Chrysothemis' observation and deduction is that she 'knows' (907, 923) that Orestes has returned. This knowledge brings joy with it as an appropriate emotional accompaniment (871-4, 906, 921, 934). Electra thinks that Chrysothemis' mental processes are defective (879, 920, 922), and that her euphoria is therefore deluded (891). Chrysothemis can only reiterate 'How can I not know what I saw clearly?' (923). Electra rejects her story on the basis of what she herself heard 'from one who was present when Orestes died' (927). Chrysothemis is thus brought to accept that her joy was after all based on ignorance, and that she has found new sufferings on top of the ones she had before (934-6).

The second half of the act introduces a theme which does not occur in Aeschylus' *Libation Bearers* or Euripides' *Electra* but which is characteristic of Sophocles. There is a close parallel with the first act (*prologos*) of *Antigone*, where Antigone tries to persuade her sister Ismene to join in her plan to bury their brother Polynices. Electra proposes to Chrysothemis that, now Orestes is dead, the two of them together should kill Aegisthus

(955-7; cf. 1001). This proposal is discussed more fully in Chapter 5. Electra argues that they now have nothing to look forward to but living out their lives as spinsters, robbed of their father's wealth and with no prospect of marriage. But if Electra's plan succeeds, they will not only have shown piety to their father and brother, but will gain honour, glory, and good marriages. Electra repeatedly uses the Greek dual form as she strives to bind her sister to her to make an inseparable pair. Chrysothemis rejects Electra's plan as impracticable, since she is a woman (cf. *Antigone* 61-2) and their enemies are much stronger (cf. *Antigone* 63-4, 79). Such an attempt would lead only to a disgraceful death and the extinction of the family (cf. *Antigone* 58-60). Electra despises her sister's timidity, and resolves to carry out the plan herself (cf. *Antigone* 69-72). The argument, as in their earlier scene, is now conducted in angry stichomythia. Electra even challenges Chrysothemis to go and inform Clytemnestra of her plan (cf. *Antigone* 86). On this occasion, however, there is no rapprochement. Chrysothemis exits into the palace at the end of the act, with the taunt that Electra will come in time to see the wisdom of her words. This is a much harsher conclusion than Ismene's final words in the first act of *Antigone*: 'Go, then, if you must; and of this be sure, – that, though your errand is foolish, to your dear ones you are truly dear' (*Antigone* 98-9, trans. Jebb, slightly adapted). Electra, left with no prospect of help from anyone, remains on stage during the ode which the chorus now sings.

Second choral ode (second *stasimon*) 1058-97

This is the second of only three choral odes in the play, all of them quite short. It is an encomium (= formal praise) of Electra for her piety in choosing a life of mourning for Agamemnon. The encomium was a well-established genre in Greek poetry, notable examples being the odes in praise of victorious athletes by Pindar (*c.* 518 – *c.* 438 BC). Encomiastic odes are quite common in Euripides (e.g. *Alcestis* 435-75, *Andromache* 766-801), but this is the only surviving example in Sophocles. This type of poetry has a stock vocabulary of terms of commendation, which gain resonance from constant repetition in one poem after another.

The second *strophê* of this ode is rich in such terms: 'No one who is noble would want to disgrace a good reputation by living basely and ingloriously, my child, my child. Thus you have chosen a splendid life of mourning, overcoming dishonour so as to win at once a twofold praise, to be called both wise and best of daughters' (1082-9).[5] The word *agathos*, translated here as 'noble', is the basic Greek word for 'good'. When used of persons it can also imply bravery and moral goodness, as well as abilities of other kinds. The *agathos* will also be *sophos* ('wise', 1089; cf. Euripides, *Alcestis* 603). The idea in encomiastic contexts is that all these qualities are connected. The superlative of *agathos* is *aristos* ('best', 1089, 1097), and its opposite is *kakos* ('base', cf. 1083). This vocabulary has strong aristocratic connotations, and the implication here is that Electra has inherited the nobility of her distinguished father (1089). She is *eupatris* ('noble daughter of a noble father', 1081), as Orestes is *eupatridês*, the masculine equivalent (162, 858). The *agathos* strives to be *kleinos* ('splendid', 1086) and to gain *eukleia* ('good reputation', 1083). It is somewhat paradoxical that Electra achieves this by choosing a 'life of mourning' (1085-6). Glory is immortal, and the *agathos* will prefer death to shame (cf. 1078-9). The chorus hopes, however, that Electra will get the upper hand over her enemies and be restored to the wealth and power which are appropriate to the *agathos* (1090-2).

The meaning of the second half of the ode is thus clear enough, despite one or two problems of detail. The first half is somewhat more difficult. The chorus asks why we do not show the same care for our parents as birds do for theirs. The Greeks regarded storks as being especially admirable in this respect (cf. Aristophanes, *Birds* 1355-7). The chorus goes on to swear by the lightning-flash of Zeus and by Themis (goddess of justice) that we shall otherwise not long be free from trouble. Some scholars have thought that this is an indirect criticism of Chrysothemis' refusal to help Electra. This is impossible. In the first place, the chorus' previous utterance was to express approval of her sensible advice to Electra (1015-16). Secondly, this solemn threat is out of all proportion to any offence committed by the timid and gentle Chrysothemis. Thirdly, she has just returned from placing offerings on her father's grave, so can hardly be accused now of neglecting her parents.

The key to understanding the structure of this ode is to grasp that Greek choral lyric regularly proceeds from the general to the particular. The chorus' observations in the first eight lines of the ode are thus expressed in quite general terms. Choruses can start at some distance from their eventual destination. Secondly, choruses often begin with a 'foil', that is to say something which contrasts strongly with their main point and thereby gives emphasis to it. An ode in the *Antigone* thus begins 'Happy are they whose life has never tasted suffering' (582), although the subject of the ode is the unhappy house of Labdacus. There is no need to ask which particular happy people the chorus has in mind. In some cases, the foil may be broadly applicable to something in the play, while not being a specific reference to it. In Euripides' *Andromache*, the chorus introduces its praise of Peleus by saying: 'It is better not to have disreputable victory than to overthrow justice invidiously and violently. For this is sweet at first for mortals, but in time it withers away and the house is involved in disgrace' (779-84). These lines have some general relevance to the behaviour of Menelaus earlier in the play, but they do not refer specifically to him. Their function is to set off the feats of Peleus which the chorus goes on to praise. Similarly in this ode in *Electra*, the chorus' approval of Electra ought logically to imply some disapproval of Chrysothemis — if not necessarily as strong as that expressed here — but these opening lines are significantly phrased in general terms. The lines which follow (1066-73) also function as a foil. The chorus prays that news of the troubles in Agamemnon's house should be conveyed to him in the underworld as a reproach. These troubles are the dark background to the shining virtue of his daughter Electra.

Fifth act (third *epeisodion*) 1098-1383

Orestes and Pylades enter by an *eisodos*. They are accompanied by attendants carrying a funerary urn (1123). It is not clear whether they use the same *eisodos* by which they departed at line 85, the one which will now be associated with the way to Agamemnon's grave. This staging would give the impression that they have returned directly from the grave, as Orestes earlier said that they would do (53) and as Chrysothemis did earlier. It is perhaps more likely that they use the *eisodos* by which they entered at the beginning of the play, and by which the Paedagogus entered at line 660. This *eisodos* would then be associated with travellers arriving from a distance, as Orestes and Pylades purport to be doing here. We have no direct evidence that the two *eisodoi* were systematically differentiated in the fifth-century theatre, let alone how they were used in a particular play, but the potential dramatic significance of a distinction between them can hardly be overlooked.

This act is mostly devoted to the recognition of Orestes and Electra. Such recognition scenes were popular in fifth-century drama, and they were elaborated with increasing complexity and sophistication. Euripides was especially fond of them, and there are examples in his *Electra, Iphigenia among the Taurians, Ion*, and *Helen*. The earliest surviving example in drama is in Aeschylus' *Libation Bearers*, but there is already a sequence of recognition scenes in Homer's *Odyssey* which establishes many features of the genre. Odysseus repeatedly delays making himself known to his loved ones, even when there can be no possible danger in doing so. The result is to prolong the suffering of his wife Penelope and his father Laertes. One reason for this is that he must be allowed time to gain a full understanding of what his family has been suffering for so long in his absence, and this can best be derived from seeing their condition before they realize that he has returned. We see him see them suffer, and the ironic and emotional power of this outweighs the implausibility of his allowing their suffering to continue longer than might seem necessary.

Homer also pioneered the devices by which recognition is finally achieved. Odysseus' old nurse Eurycleia recognizes him when she touches a scar on his leg (*Odyssey* 19.392-3), and he later shows this scar to Eumaeus and Philoetius as proof of his identity (*Odyssey* 21.217-20). In Euripides' *Electra*, Orestes is similarly identified by a scar, located more visibly on his forehead (573-4). Penelope recognizes Odysseus because he can describe the construction of their bed (*Odyssey* 23.205-6). A similar display of privileged knowledge by Orestes convinces his sister Iphigenia of his identity in Euripides' *Iphigenia among the Taurians* (811-26). The third main recognition device is the possession of a distinctive object. Orestes finally convinces Electra of his identity in Sophocles' *Electra* by showing her Agamemnon's signet ring (1222-3), and in Aeschylus' *Libation Bearers* by producing an example of her weaving (231-2).

The chorus directs Orestes to Electra as a suitable person to announce his arrival because she is 'next of kin' to those inside (1105). She responds by expressing apprehension about his news, and then grief when he reveals that he has brought Orestes' ashes. Jebb (note on line 1106) was convinced that Orestes identifies Electra immediately here, observing that earlier he had no difficulty in recognizing her voice (80). Sophocles actually gives no hint (e.g. through an aside) that he has recognized her, yet it is remarkable that he should be so uninterested in the identity of this grief-stricken well-wisher. He gives Electra the urn, speculating that she must be 'a friend or relation' of the dead man (1125). Such ironies are common in recognition scenes, but Orestes' behaviour here is unusually difficult to interpret. Some scholars have suggested that Electra is unrecognizable because she has been worn out by grief and suffering, and that Orestes expected his sister to be of more obviously noble appearance. Friedrich Solmsen thus writes of Orestes' failure to recognize Electra previously: 'He could not in this woman worn out by grief and suffering, prematurely aged and of neglected appearance find anything like the *kleinon eidos* [illustrious form] of his sister. Evidently he had thought of her as a radiant figure; although he knew in general terms about

55

her unhappy condition, his imagination had been unable to visualize anything like the truth now before him'.[6] This is made more explicit by Hofmannsthal's Orestes: 'Electra must be / ten years younger than you. Electra is tall, / her eye is sad but gentle whereas yours / is full of blood and hatred' (cf. Chapter 7). So far as Sophocles is concerned, however, this would be as much of an imaginative construct as Jebb's theory that Orestes identified her immediately, and Sophocles gives us equally little encouragement to accept it. All one can say for the moment is that Orestes' impassivity here is consistent with his detachment from Electra for most of the play, and shows the extremes to which Sophocles will go in delaying their recognition. Orestes was easily deflected by the Paedagogus from his impulse to listen to Electra's lament (80-2), he does not involve her in his plot, and shows no interest in how she might react to a report of his death.

The chorus addresses Electra by name after her lament over the urn, and Orestes then gives the first explicit indication that he has identified her. Most scholars suppose that he has gradually realized who she is during her lament, although it has been argued that he does not do so until he actually hears her name (1171). It requires a further 50 lines of dialogue before she finally identifies him (1224). This dialogue is in the form of stichomythia, also prominent in the recognitions in Aeschylus' *Libation Bearers* (212-24) and Euripides' *Electra* (547-81). Stichomythia, with its rapidly evolving interplay between two characters and its scope for cryptic questions and exclamations, is ideally suited to this type of scene. The recognition culminates in a sequence of *antilabe*, in which a line of verse is divided between two speakers (1220-6). Orestes formally identifies himself by showing Electra the signet ring of Agamemnon, but this technical proof is only the culmination of the affinity which has developed between them during the whole dialogue. The verbal interplay is accompanied by action, as Orestes struggles to take the urn from Electra. He asks her to give it to him at 1205, but she still has it at 1216 and we can only be sure that she has relinquished it when she embraces him at 1226. Orestes presumably takes it and gives it to one of his attendants.

The reunion of Orestes and Electra is followed by a 'recognition duo' (1232-87).[7] Such duos were favoured by Euripides towards the end of his career, and there are four surviving examples in his later plays, all probably close in date to *Electra* (e.g. *Iphigenia among the Taurians* 827-99, *Helen* 625-97). This is the only surviving example in Sophocles, and there can be little doubt that he has adopted the form from Euripides. The male character is always the more restrained in these scenes, and performs almost entirely in iambic trimeters (the metre of the spoken parts of tragedy). The female character is more emotional, and performs wholly or mainly in lyrics (especially dochmiacs, the most agitated of the lyric metres). This contrast is central to the effect of these scenes, but normally the male character does at least join in to some extent with the female's joy. This scene is exceptional in that Orestes repeatedly tries to suppress Electra's euphoric outbursts in case they are overheard by their enemies inside the palace. This may seem sensible in realistic terms, but dramatic convention allowed such caution to be postponed until the joy of reunion has been fully expressed. Orestes' businesslike attitude can only recall his earlier lack of alertness to Electra and her feelings. He gives up trying to restrain her towards the end of the duo, but Jenny March exaggerates a little when she says that he 'emphasises his own emotional response to Electra's feelings' and 'reassures her that his joy is no less than hers' (p. 213). March translates the relevant line: 'ELECTRA: Do you feel as I do? ORESTES: Of course I do!' (1280).

Recognition is followed, as usual in such scenes, by the formulation of a plot (1288-1383). Orestes tells Electra to spare him details of the usurpers' wickedness, but rather to give practical advice on defeating them. Electra replies that Aegisthus is away but that Clytemnestra is in the palace, and promises that she will not betray her joy in her features. Orestes then hears someone coming out of the palace, and tells Electra to be quiet. She adroitly pretends to be in the process of ushering the strangers into the palace. The Paedagogus, rather than the expected enemy, comes out. He rebukes Orestes and Electra for indulging in lengthy conversation and insatiable cries of joy, and presses upon them the urgent need for action. This is rather odd. It is entirely normal for a call to action to follow the celebration of reunion. This happens in Aeschylus' *Libation Bearers* (510-13) and Euripides' *Electra* (596-604), but is as old as Homer's *Odyssey* (21.226-41). The difference here is that Orestes and Electra have already concluded the recognition duo and turned their attention to plotting. Orestes, indeed, has just asked Electra for information about the situation inside the palace which was supposed to have been supplied by the Paedagogus (39-41). The Paedagogus at any rate brings an added sense of urgency. Before they go in, Orestes needs to remind Electra who the Paedagogus is and she greets him effusively (1354-63).

The Paedagogus then says 'Now is the time (*kairos*) to act; now Clytemnestra is alone; now no man is inside' (1368-9). The avengers focus for the first time specifically on Clytemnestra, but even here it is not stated in so many words that Orestes intends to kill her. His entrance into the palace seals his decision, but he has never once expressed awareness of what that decision entails. Sophocles conspicuously omits the phrase 'kill my mother' which defines his awareness of the horror of his deed in Aeschylus (*Libation Bearers* 899) and Euripides (*Electra* 967). Orestes offers a brief prayer as the three men depart into the palace. Electra remains to add a prayer to Apollo, an echo of Clytemnestra's earlier prayer to him. She too then goes in, the first time that she has left the stage since she entered 1300 lines earlier. Her wait is over.

Third choral ode (third *stasimon*) 1384-97

This brief ode consists of one strophic pair. Sophocles hurries to the climax of the play, and the chorus maintains suspense as Orestes advances against Clytemnestra. The avengers are envisaged as Furies, 'the hounds that none can escape, pursuers of evil deeds'. Burton remarks on the metre of this ode, 'in whose rhythms one can almost hear the sound of footsteps' (p. 215). They are actually rather vigorous footsteps (di-di-di dum, di-di-di dum, di-di-di dum), perhaps recalling the use of the same metre to describe the Furies leaping on their victims in Aeschylus' *Eumenides* (372-6). Orestes is 'the champion of the dead and the gods below'. Hermes, god of deception, leads him on to the end.

This ode is closely linked with the first *stasimon* (472-515), where the chorus expressed confidence that Clytemnestra's dream portended disaster for her and that Justice and a Fury would come to punish her. Their vision seems now to be becoming a reality.

Sixth act (*exodos*) 1398-1510

The last act of the play is divided into two parts, the first dealing with the death of Clytemnestra and the second with that of Aegisthus.

The first part begins with Electra rushing out of the palace to watch out for Aegisthus. She describes the scene within, and Clytemnestra's death cries are heard. Greek tragedy tended to avoid showing violence and death on stage, and murder always takes place off stage. Sometimes someone is killed inside the stage building, and the death cries are heard from within. The earliest surviving example is in Aeschylus' *Agamemnon* (1343-6), and Agamemnon's death cries are exactly repeated here by Clytemnestra ('Ah! I am struck ... Ah! For a second time!'). It is also common for characters on stage to comment on the death cries. Electra exhorts Orestes to strike a second time, and the chorus reacts briefly to Clytemnestra's death. Orestes and Pylades enter, and the chorus comments 'A bloodstained hand drips with a sacrifice to Ares, and I cannot fault it' (1422-3). Orestes confirms that Clytemnestra is dead, but further discussion of the deed is curtailed by the chorus' announcement of the approach of Aegisthus. Electra and the chorus send Orestes and Pylades back into the palace.

59

This complex and exciting scene is arranged in a strict formal structure. It takes the form of a strophic pair containing a mixture of iambic trimeters and lyrics (1398-1441). The *antistrophê* begins with the entrance of Orestes and Pylades. Burton writes: 'All these comings and goings, cries "off", alarms, and quick exchanges between speakers and singers are controlled by the laws of rhythmical symmetry and exact responsion in the division of lines' (p. 223). Burton remarks that Sophocles generally preferred to organize lyric dialogue into strophic pairs. Euripides, by contrast, made increasing use of free lyric dialogue.

Aegisthus enters by an *eisodos* in search of the Phocian strangers, so that he can receive confirmation of the death of Orestes. He addresses Electra brusquely, and she replies with a series of ambiguous utterances. He demands to see the body of Orestes, which he assumes to be in the palace. He orders that the doors of the palace be opened, so that all the Argives can see that there is no longer any hope of liberation by Orestes. In theatrical terms, this is a conventional prompt for the appearance of the *ekkyklêma*. It is not always clear when the *ekkyklêma* is being used, but it is usually supposed that the corpses of Clytemnestra and Aegisthus were displayed on it in Aeschylus' *Libation Bearers*. Here, the *ekkyklêma* brings out a covered corpse, accompanied by Orestes and Pylades in their guise as Phocian strangers. Aegisthus uncovers it, and is horrified to discover that it is the corpse of Clytemnestra. He immediately realizes that the stranger is Orestes, and that he is doomed. Electra exhorts Orestes to kill him as quickly as possible. Orestes has a brief dialogue with him before taking him into the palace, accompanied as always by Pylades. Electra presumably follows.

The chorus utters the final words of the play: 'Seed of Atreus, after so many sufferings you have emerged at last in freedom, fulfilled by this day's enterprise' (1508-10). The chorus then departs by an *eisodos*.

4

Stagecraft

Sophocles was one of the greatest masters of the medium in the history of theatre, and *Electra* exemplifies many aspects of his skill as a dramatist. Several of these were mentioned in Chapter 3, but some topics deserve more co-ordinated discussion. In particular, he makes sophisticated use of tragic conventions which would have been familiar to his audience. *Electra* cannot be understood without some grasp of them.

Sophocles' plays always have a detailed topography, in which the relatively small area represented by the stage is placed in a larger context. This context can include both the immediate environment and more remote places. In *Electra*, the more immediate offstage locations are the interior of the palace of the Pelopidae and the city of Mycenae. The significance of these places needs to be considered. Two more distant places are also relevant. The first is Phocis, where Pylades was born and brought up and where Orestes has lived in exile. They pretend to be visitors from there, as does the Paedagogus. The second is Delphi (in the same part of Greece), the location of the famous oracle of Apollo and of the Pythian games which are described at length in the messenger speech.

In considering a Greek tragedy, we should always bear in mind the distinction between what the audience sees and what it hears about. The use of narrative to convey information about offstage events is especially striking in the messenger speech, a stock feature of Greek tragedy. Messengers conventionally tell the truth, so it is remarkable that the Paedagogus should deliver a speech which gives every appearance of being a messenger speech but which is in fact an elaborate deception. One of Sophocles' most famous props is the urn which ostensibly contains Orestes' ashes. The fictitious messenger speech has its visual analogue in the empty urn over which Electra laments.

Finally, some observations will be made about the role of the chorus, with particular reference to the authority of the choral 'voice'. The contributions of the chorus were discussed individually in Chapter 3, but the aim now will be to summarize their effect on the overall tone and meaning of the play. The chorus supports Electra and favours the revenge, and it is necessary to have some understanding of the conventional role of the chorus in Greek tragedy if one is to understand the significance of this.

The palace of the Pelopidae

The earliest surviving tragedy in which the *skênê* (stage building) plays a significant dramatic part is Aeschylus' *Agamemnon* (458 BC). The *skênê* represents a particular place, usually a building, in all later surviving tragedies. The *skênê* is the backdrop to the action, and its main door is one of the ways by which actors make their entrances and exits. In most tragedies, the *skênê* represents a place where crucial events happen before and during the time of the action. Its main door will often be the focus of attention.

P.E. Easterling observes that the *skênê* in *Electra* represents 'the famous House of the Pelopidae, immensely grand, rich and sinister ... This is where Agamemnon was murdered by his own wife, where the evil usurpers now live, perverting all civilised norms, where during the play itself Clytemnestra will be killed and Aegisthus driven to his death'.[1] The Paedagogus describes the house as 'rich in gold' (9; cf. 1393), but also as 'rich in slaughter' (10), alluding to the many murders known to have taken place there even before that of Agamemnon. Orestes was stolen away into exile from this murderous scene, and he returns to it at the beginning of the play. The chorus remarks that 'grievous violence' has never yet left the house since the death of Myrtilus (514-15). Aegisthus predicts that the house will witness 'the present and the future woes of the Pelopidae' (1497-8).

The building is now 'the house of Aegisthus' (660-2, 1101-2), where he spends Agamemnon's wealth, sits on his throne, wears his regalia, and sleeps with his wife (266-74, 1290-1). The usurpers are 'those inside' (821). The house is the source of political power in Mycenae. Clytemnestra dreamed that Agamemnon planted his sceptre at its hearth, from which it sent forth a branch which overshadowed the whole city (417-23). Orestes prays that he be received back into the house as the restorer of its fortunes, since he has come in justice as 'a purifier sent by the gods' (67-72). He expresses his decision to kill Clytemnestra as one to 'go inside' (1374), and the chorus then sings of Orestes and Pylades as Furies who have passed into the house (1384-97).

The door is the point of transition between the outside world and this perverse and violent interior. Electra is normally confined within, and is only able to come out now because Aegisthus is away in the country (312-13, 517-20). She repeatedly complains that she must share this building with her father's murderers and that she is treated by them as a slave (190-2, 256-65). She expresses her grief before the door for all to hear (109; cf. 328, 802), and eventually decides to waste away her life there and never go back inside (817-22). She brings out into public view what Clytemnestra would prefer to be concealed (cf. 641-2).

The overthrow of the usurpers is associated with a breakdown of the boundary between inside and outside. This process begins with the Paedagogus listening from inside to the all-too-audible reunion of Orestes and Electra (1331-8). There is then the remarkable scene in which Electra stands at the door, and commentates on the murder of Clytemnestra taking place inside (1398-1421). Aegisthus throws open the door so that all the Mycenaeans and Argives can see what is within (1458-9). Finally, he is taken in to be killed, and the doors are closed once more.

The city of Mycenae

The play begins with the Paedagogus pointing out to Orestes
the features of the local landscape. He indicates the plain of
Argos; the marketplace dedicated to Apollo in Argos, in reality
six miles to the south; and, 'here on the left', the famous temple
of Hera (the 'Argive Heraeum'), in reality two miles to the south
east and not actually visible from Mycenae at all. Sophocles
seems to have collapsed the distance between these places in
order to create a synthetic Mycenae-Argos which combines the
features of both (see Jebb's note on lines 4-8). Orestes' country
is 'the famous land of the Mycenaeans' (160-2) but he himself is
described as 'Argive' (693). Aegisthus describes the people as
'Mycenaeans and Argives' (1459). Mycenae, ruined by the time
of the first performance of *Electra* and long insignificant, would
have lacked the familiar landmarks necessary to the strong
sense of place evoked here.

   Bernard Knox comments on this opening speech by the
Paedagogus: 'Such a prologue seems the appropriate opening
note for a drama which will emphasize the political aspect of
Orestes' action: the overthrow of a tyranny, the restoration of
freedom.'[2] Knox himself actually believes that Sophocles
focusses on the domestic theme, but other scholars have found
rather more political significance in the play. Aegisthus sits on
Agamemnon's throne and wears his regalia (267-9). Agamemnon's sceptre figures prominently in Clytemnestra's dream as a
symbol of power over Mycenae (420), and she prays that she will
continue to wield it (651). She is afraid that Electra will spread
malicious rumours 'through the whole *polis*' (642). The Paedagogus refers to Aegisthus as a *tyrannos*, or absolute ruler (661,
664). Aegisthus makes clear at the end of the play that there is
opposition to his rule which centres on hopes for Orestes' return. He demands that Orestes' supposed corpse be displayed:
'I tell you to open the doors, and display the sight to all the
Mycenaeans and Argives; so that if any of them were once
excited by empty hopes because of this man, they will now see
his corpse and accept my bridle, instead of waiting for punish-

ment from me to make them wise against their will' (1458-63). The chorus of free-born women of Mycenae gives a broader social context to the action than do the household slaves in Aeschylus' *Libation Bearers*, even if it is a less narrowly political context than it might have been had it consisted of men. Electra addresses them with a rare term which may be translated 'women of the *polis*' or 'citizen women' (1227).[3] When Clytemnestra is being killed, the chorus briefly considers the fate of the city as well as of the race of Pelops (1413).

Knox argues, by contrast, that these references to the *polis* do not amount to much, and that attention is focussed on the family. Even when Electra fantasizes about the glory which she and Chrysothemis will win from killing Aegisthus, she imagines it being said that they 'saved their father's house' (978) rather than that they freed the city. Knox observes that 'freedom' in *Electra* is always personal freedom (339, 970, 1256, 1300), most notably in the last lines of the play, where it is the family rather than the city on whose liberation the chorus comments. Knox contrasts this personal and domestic emphasis in Sophocles with the importance of the political theme in Aeschylus' *Libation Bearers* and Euripides' *Electra*. Jasper Griffin has similarly drawn attention to the unpolitical character of the play. He remarks that 'Electra mourns Agamemnon not as a political figure, a rightful king assassinated and replaced by a usurper, but as her father, pitifully dead' (citing 95, 115, 133, 341, 399, etc.).[4] He observes that Orestes pays more attention to Agamemnon's property than to his kingship (1290-2, 1391-3).

The play is thus firmly located in the context of the *polis* of Mycenae-Argos. There are also a number of references which bring out the political implications of the action as the overthrow of a tyranny. On the other hand, Knox and Griffin are right that the political significance of the action is played down. The reason for this apparent contradiction may be that it is specifically Electra who views events in personal and familial terms. She would be a very different character if she had a wider sense of the significance of her struggle. The chorus largely reflects and amplifies her feelings. The play may indeed be dominated by Electra's passionate subjectivity, but Sophocles does not allow the audience entirely to ignore the political context.

The messenger speech

In Aeschylus' *Libation Bearers*, Orestes himself brings the false news of his death. He arrives in the guise of a stranger from Phocis, and says that he encountered Strophius on his way. He says that Strophius told him that Orestes is dead, and that he awaits instructions about the disposal of the ashes. No details are volunteered about how Orestes died. Clytemnestra expresses grief, and invites Orestes and Pylades into the palace. Electra is probably not present. The whole scene occupies 66 lines, and Orestes' lying speech a mere 17 lines (674-90).

In *Electra*, the false news of Orestes' death is brought by the Paedagogus, who elaborates his story in an 84-line speech. It is a major problem in the play why Sophocles should have devoted so much space to a long and exciting speech in which there is apparently not a word of truth (see MacLeod, pp. 108-10 for a brief survey of discussions). One explanation is that the circumstantial detail contributes to the plausibility of the story, and thus ensures that Clytemnestra will be off her guard when Orestes arrives (e.g. March, note on lines 680-763). This is true as far as it goes, but Clytemnestra is not portrayed as being especially sceptical, and Sophocles was free to have her convinced by a less elaborate story.

Another line of interpretation has been to look for some truth behind the fictitious details of the Paedagogus' story. The Orestes whom he describes is a glittering figure, winning a series of victories at one of Greece's most prestigious games. The Paedagogus remarks 'I know of no one whose deeds and triumphs are the match of his' (689). It is intrinsically plausible that the son of the great Agamemnon should be capable of such glorious feats. Charles Segal writes of Orestes' 'involvement in the competitive male world, with its brightness ..., throngs,

sudden vicissitudes, as opposed to the actionless, dark, invo-
luted world of Electra'.[5] Blundell sees more of a contrast
between fiction and reality, arguing that the heroic Orestes of
the messenger speech is at odds with the ruthless intriguer that
we see in the play (pp. 173-4). Orestes' chariot race recalls that
of Pelops which was mentioned in the previous ode (504-15) as
being the origin of the house's troubles. Other scholars have
speculated whether Orestes' reported death may have some
sinister significance, a possibility which Orestes himself rejected (59-66). David Seale suggested that 'the audience [may]
be meant to take from this mass of fabrication the truth that
the "heroic" Orestes has in fact died' (p. 66). Winnington-
Ingram thought that Orestes really did suffer disaster
through his connexion with Delphi, not by being killed at the
games there but by obeying the command of the Delphic
oracle to kill his mother. The truth turns out to be worse than
the lie (pp. 236-7).

There is certainly precedent in Greek literature for lies which
contain an element of truth. The most famous examples are the
lying tales which Odysseus tells in the *Odyssey*. Odysseus
depends for his survival on his skill at deception, and Homer
uses these lies to broaden the scope of the poem. Richard
Rutherford observes: 'The "lies" are not composed out of pure
imagination. They include details relevant to the addressee,
they present from a different slant important themes of the
poem ..., and they echo or reflect various adventures experienced by Odysseus or his fellow heroes.'[6] Sophocles too was
interested in lying tales which contain an element of truth.
Ajax's 'trick speech' (*Ajax* 646-92) is most plausibly explained
as a deliberate deception which nevertheless expresses profound truths about the world. Lichas gives Deianira a
misleading account of Heracles' activities which contains a good
deal of truth (*Women of Trachis* 248-90), and there is a similar
blend of truth and fiction in the deceptive tales in *Philoctetes*
(343-90, 539-627).

A particular problem with the Paedagogus' speech is that he
fulfils the conventional role of the 'messenger' in tragedy. The

messenger is an anonymous lower-status character who delivers a long speech describing an important offstage event. The great majority of extant tragedies contain a 'messenger speech', so the formal conventions were well-established. The term 'messenger' is actually a misnomer, since this type of character brings news rather than a message. The messenger normally begins with an unspecific indication that his news will be bad (e.g. Euripides, *Hippolytus* 1157-9), so it is striking that the Paedagogus begins here by announcing that his news will be good (666-7). The messenger then gives his news in brief (cf. 673), before giving a long speech in response to a request for details (cf. 678-9). The messenger typically concludes by commenting on the tragic nature of the events which he has described (cf. 761-3).

The messenger-speech, with its set-piece description enlivened by directly quoted speech, has obvious formal and stylistic resemblances to epic poetry (especially Homer's *Iliad* and *Odyssey*). It has often been supposed that the messenger also shares with the epic narrator a certain omniscience and objectivity, offering unemotional and undistorted access to the truth. This belief in the transparency of the messenger-speech has been challenged, notably by Irene de Jong in a book which employs modern narratology to detect subtleties of characterization and 'focalization' which serve to locate the messenger as an individual inside the drama.[7] James Barrett has, however, reaffirmed the objectivity and self-effacement of the messenger, and stressed his appropriation of the authority of the epic narrator.[8] This narrative voice is by definition trustworthy, and the messenger would lose much of his usefulness to the poet if he were unreliable. Barrett offers an interesting comparison with Homer's description of the chariot race in the *Iliad*, where there is disagreement among the spectators about what is happening (23.362-538). The Paedagogus, by contrast, offers a comprehensive account of the race, with confident description both of the overall picture and of close-up details. His narrative is only intelligible in terms of the privileged knowledge of the tragic messenger. No one disbelieves a messenger speech in tragedy, so it is not surprising that Clytemnestra and Electra are convinced. The Paedagogus' speech is thus a lying narrative which dramatic convention indicates to be truthful. Barrett argues that this alerts us to the devices which give plausibility to all messenger speeches, and reminds us that even a messenger speech which is truthful within the fictive world of the play is untruthful from the point of view of the audience. He thinks that this is an aspect of the play's 'metatheatricality', that is to say its self-consciousness about its status as drama. That may be the case, but the Paedagogus' speech remains exceptional in being untruthful within the drama, and the meaning of this needs to be considered.

There has been much discussion of the extent to which spectators are taken in by the Paedagogus' speech. Winnington-Ingram writes: 'One has heard it stated and denied with equal vehemence by spectators (and readers) that disbelief is involuntarily suspended by the power of the narrative, i.e. that they react emotionally as though it were true. The matter is not worth arguing: some people react one way, some another' (p. 236 n. 66). On the contrary, these conflicting views represent responses to something specific in the play. This is not just a matter of any or all of the spectators literally forgetting for a greater or lesser length of time that the Paedagogus is not telling the truth. A spectator who reacts to the speech as though it were true is not being naïvely forgetful, but is showing a competent grasp of dramatic convention. The speech is characterized as a messenger speech, and is thus marked as truthful. Sophocles could not do more to make spectators believe something that they know to be false. He implicates the audience in one of the main themes of the play, the relationship between subjective conviction and objective truth. This cannot be separated from the issue of the matricide itself, and Sophocles' arrangement of the play in such a way that it is almost exclusively dominated by Electra's passionate belief in the justice of the revenge.

The urn

The urn supposedly containing Orestes' ashes is mentioned briefly in Aeschylus (*Libation Bearers* 686-7), but does not appear on stage. In *Electra*, it features in the plot (54-5), is mentioned again at the end of the messenger speech (757-8), and is finally brought on to the stage (1098). Some scholars see a further allusion to the jug containing libations which Electra carries at the beginning of Aeschylus' *Libation Bearers*. This scene seems to have been popular with vase painters, and would have been well-known to Sophocles' audience. Euripides' Electra is also associated with a vessel, the water-pot which she carries on her head when she enters (Euripides, *Electra* 54). One might have expected these various vessels to be somewhat different in shape, which would make the allusion less obvious. It must be admitted, however, that the dramatists are flexible in their terminology, and the basic similarity between these vessels may be the main thing. Sophocles and Euripides would thus exploit the resonances of the classic image of the tragic Electra with her urn, while also advertising what is distinctive of their own treatments. Aeschylus' Electra carries a vessel for ritual purposes, Euripides' Electra performs the secular and mundane task of fetching water, while Sophocles' Electra delivers an impassioned but deluded lament.

Electra's lament over the urn (1126-70) is the climax not only of her suffering but also of her delusion. On the one hand, it expresses profound grief, and is indeed one of the most powerful of all tragic laments. On the other hand, the urn is empty, and the living Orestes is standing beside her. Brian Vickers writes: 'We see Electra's suffering but we do not share it, since it is not real, it could be dispelled at any moment.'[9] It is evident that Electra's lament raises similar questions to the messenger speech, in that its verbal power conflicts with the audience's knowledge that it is based on falsehood. This is hardly an accident or evidence of Sophocles' incompetence, but an aspect of the systematic way in which he sets subjective conviction at odds with objective truth.

Charles Segal sees metatheatrical significance in the urn as a symbol of tragedy. It is an elaborate work of art, but there are no real human remains in it. The contents of the urn have been conjured up by words, especially the Paedagogus' messenger speech. The audience invests emotion in the play, as Electra does in the urn. 'Like Electra, too, the audience must be able to put aside the fictive envelope, the false and deceptive vessel, and turn back to the true forms of the living world when the fiction has done its work.'[10] This ingenious interpretation, like Barrett's metatheatrical reading of the messenger speech, seems to underplay the very specific challenge which Sophocles poses to our responses in this particular play.

The urn is the focus of a notable piece of stagecraft (1205-26, discussed in Chapter 3) when Orestes manages with difficulty to take the urn from Electra. We last hear of it as Clytemnestra decks it for burial, immediately before she is killed (1400-1).

The chorus

Choral singing and dancing was a prestigious element of Greek culture from an early period. Many examples survive of choral poetry in various genres (e.g. hymns, victory-odes, dithyrambs). The City Dionysia, at which the tragedies were performed, also featured twenty dithyrambs with a total of 1000 performers. In historical terms, tragedy seems to have grown out of choral performance, and the chorus plays a correspondingly larger part in the earlier extant tragedies. The role of the chorus gradually declined in the course of the fifth century, and by the fourth century seems to have been reduced to providing interludes with little or no dramatic relevance. The chorus is still dramatically important in Sophocles, and delivers about 15% of the total number of lines in *Electra*.

The power of the choral voice in Greek culture brought with it both opportunities and problems for the dramatist.[11] Tragic choruses can express themselves in a distinctively choral style which locates their utterances in the rich tradition of Greek choral poetry. All choruses have a family resemblance which

71

transcends their dramatic identity in a particular play. This choral style is often abstract and high-flown, allowing for memorable expression of moral and religious ideas in dense and suggestive language. Choral odes can draw on well-established genres such as the encomium *panegyric* (e.g. *Electra* 1058-97) and the hymn (e.g. *Antigone* 100-54). This choral voice gives the chorus' utterances an authority which goes well beyond that of the group in their fictive identity, and allows the dramatist to expand the scope of the play and give resonance to the action. A problem was that there could be a danger of the chorus overpowering other voices in a play. Sophocles, more than most dramatists, avoided expounding 'the meaning of the play' in any explicit way. His plays have a certain inscrutability. He thus undermines the authority of the chorus, for example by subordinating it to a character whose own position is questionable or partial. Choruses can be inconsistent or mistaken, and make forceful statements whose relevance is obscure.

The tragic chorus always has a specific identity and location in the world of the play. *Electra* has a chorus of Mycenaean women who are broadly sympathetic to Electra, and their opinions and attitudes reflect that. *Ajax* has a highly partisan chorus of Ajax's followers. The action of a tragedy may have been determined to some extent by the myth, but the poet had considerable latitude in choosing the identity of the chorus. For *Electra*, Sophocles could have chosen (e.g.) a chorus of palace slaves (as Aeschylus had done in *Libation Bearers*) or of old men with a prominent role in the public life of the *polis* (as in *Antigone*). It is worth reflecting on what effect either of those choices would have had on the overall meaning of the play.

The chorus resembles the audience in being a group which witnesses the action, tries to understand it, and survives at the end. The audience has a potential advantage over the chorus in knowing the myth, and thus how the plot may develop. The chorus has little ability to influence what happens, and this impotence is sometimes highlighted (e.g. in Aeschylus' *Agamemnon*). Choruses rarely consist of adult males in the prime of life, who were the most authoritative group in the politics of Athens as of other Greek cities. Choruses are often composed of women, slaves, or foreigners. The chorus is thus politically marginal, unlike most members of the audience, and this detracts from its ability to give authoritative expression to the values of the *polis*.

Antigone shows how Sophocles could exploit the flexibility and unreliability of the chorus. It consists of Theban elders, who are closer in gender and status to Creon than to Antigone. It tends to support Creon in the earlier part of the play (211-14, 504-5, 872-4), but turns decisively against him after he is criticized by the prophet Tiresias (1091-1107, 1270, 1347-53). It eventually makes the right judgement on him, but only after the tide of opinion (including his own) has already turned. It makes little progress towards understanding Antigone. Despite some expression of pity (801-5), it disapproves quite strongly of her (471-2, 853-6, 875), and never shows the slightest recognition that her attitude and behaviour may in any way be justified. Contrast the more sympathetic view attributed by Haemon to the people of Thebes (690-700). The chorus' flexibility is partly to be explained by the fact that it is a group, rather than an individual whose outlook might be expected to be somewhat more coherent. It can express contradictory views without offering any explicit awareness or explanation of the contradiction, e.g. in terms of a change of mind.

There is a similar flexibility in the chorus of Mycenaean women in Euripides' *Electra*. It condemns Clytemnestra's murder of Agamemnon: 'For this will the gods send death upon you as punishment. The day will come when beneath your throat I shall see your blood spilled by the sword' (483-6). Immediately after Clytemnestra has gone off to her death, it sings an ode on the justice of her punishment (1147-64). Even after her death cry, it is restrained in its expression of pity and continues to see the justice of the gods in what she is suffering (1168-71). When the blood-spattered Orestes and Electra finally appear, the chorus expresses criticisms at which they had not hinted before (1201-5, 1218-20). This change of attitude corresponds to the change of mood in Orestes and Electra themselves, and it would be misguided to ask why the chorus expressed no qualms about the matricide earlier.

The chorus in Sophocles' *Electra* consists of friends of Electra (134, 226, 307), who are hostile to Clytemnestra and Aegisthus (124-8). It addresses an encomiastic ode to her at the moment when her solitary resistance has reached its most extreme point (1058-97). The chorus helps to give full expression to the guilt of the usurpers and the suffering of Electra. It is also dramatically convenient that they should sympathize with the plot which they witness. Compare the remarkable complicity of the choruses in Euripides' *Medea* and *Orestes* with murderous plots. On the other hand, the chorus favours moderation, as choruses typically do, and regularly urges it on Electra (repeatedly in the *parodos*, and later at 369-71, 1015-16, 1171-3). It would be futile to try to assemble these various utterances into a coherent view of Electra's behaviour, and to try to explain why the chorus' opinion seems to change. The chorus is a flexible dramatic instrument, which serves to highlight what is important to the meaning of the play at any particular point. In the *parodos*, the chorus' objections bring out what is exceptional in Electra's behaviour without being an authoritative criticism of it. Later, the chorus is used to give full appreciation of Electra's remarkable defiance.

The justice of the revenge is repeatedly asserted by the chorus (173-9, 472-501, 823-5, 1384-97, 1441). Like other tragic choruses, it makes confident statements about the favour of the gods for its own side. This attitude is essentially similar to that of the chorus in the earlier part of Euripides' *Electra*. The difference is that in Sophocles the chorus never condemns the matricide. When the bloodstained Orestes emerges, it comments 'I can find no fault' (1423), before further consideration of the deed is curtailed by the arrival of Aegisthus.[12] The chorus' final words comment only on the liberation of the house of Atreus (1508-10). The chorus' support for the revenge is an apparent argument in favour of the 'affirmative' interpretation of the play, that the revenge is just. On the other hand, Sophocles' choruses never have a completely adequate understanding of the issues. They can be misguided or partisan, and can change their minds without explanation. The play ends before the murders are complete, and thus before Orestes and Electra have to face up to their consequences. There is no change of heart by Orestes for the chorus to respond to, as there is in Aeschylus' *Libation Bearers* and Euripides' *Electra*.

5

Electra

Electra is a shadowy figure in the remains of early versions of the story. The first evidence of any great interest in her is in Aeschylus, where she is prominent in the sequence from her first appearance with the libations to her recognition of Orestes (*Libation Bearers* 84-245). She does not appear in the second half of the play when the murders take place, but her brief appearance already contains much of the complex and fascinating character which would be developed by Sophocles and Euripides in their own distinctive ways. Sophocles puts her at the centre of his play. She is on stage almost throughout, and each scene is designed in terms of her interaction with another character or with the chorus. It is not surprising that some scholars have seen the play primarily as a character study.[1]

Sophocles was famous in antiquity for his portrayal of character. The ancient *Life* (21) remarked that he could 'create an entire character from a mere half-line or phrase', and he himself allegedly thought that his mature style was 'the most expressive of character and the best' (Plutarch, *Moralia* 79b). The whole question of character in Greek tragedy has been much discussed, and remains the subject of vigorous debate.[2] One point to bear in mind is that individuals in Greek tragedy have a strong tendency towards the public and the performative. Electra's lamentation is a public demonstration, not merely an expression of her inner feelings. This tendency is related both to dramatic form and to Greek views of character. A Greek tragedy comprises a variety of formal structures, which have their own integrity and momentum. An example is the iambic recapitulation of Electra's lyrics in her first speech (254-309; cf. Chapter 3). The forensic style of her speech in the agon with

Clytemnestra cannot wholly be explained in terms of character (558-609). The play has an intricate linguistic texture, from which a character cannot simply be extracted. More generally, Greek views of character focussed more on an individual's publicly accessible interaction with other people than on any hidden core of private consciousness. The emphasis is more on the ethical than the psychological, that is to say on distinctive and identifiable character traits rather than on the inner reasons why people behave as they do.

The Sophoclean hero

Each of Sophocles' seven surviving plays has a dominating individual at its centre. This individual is not necessarily on stage for the majority of the play, and may not even speak the most lines, but his or her centrality is never in doubt. Winnington-Ingram describes the Sophoclean hero as follows: 'A man or woman of excess, an extremist, obstinate, inaccessible to argument, he refuses to compromise with the conditions of human life' (p. 9). And again: 'The heroes have a dimension of greatness beyond the measure of normal humanity: they go on where ordinary men would stop. It is a kind of excess, and excess is dangerous' (p. 317). *Antigone* is the other play in which the character of this type is female, and it is the text which best illuminates *Electra*.

These heroes inevitably provoke widely diverging responses. Sophoclean critics have usefully been divided into 'hero-worshippers' and 'pietists' (cf. Winnington-Ingram, p. 322). An example of a hero-worshipper is A.F. Garvie in his edition of *Ajax*: 'Ajax falls not because he is wicked but because he is a great man, or rather because of the qualities which make him a great man.'[3] Ajax is also an extremely harsh character, vindictive to his enemies and deaf to the entreaties of his loved ones. Garvie believes that 'in rising to his full status as a hero, in transcending the limitations of ordinary human beings, he has had to forfeit some of the attractive graces of human life'.[4] Pietists, by contrast, believe that heroes are open to criticism, or even to punishment by the gods, for their excess. Sophocles gives plenty of encouragement to this type of response. Athena points to Ajax in his madness and says 'the gods love those who are sound-minded (*sôphrôn*) and hate the wicked' (*Ajax* 133). *Sôphrosunê* (adj. *sôphrôn*) is a central concept in Greek ethics, and can mean 'virtue' generally, although it essentially involves some form of self-restraint. It can thus mean 'chastity', 'self-control', 'discretion', or 'prudence' according to the context. Sophocles' heroes are notably deficient in *sôphrosunê*, at least of a conventional kind. It is always practised in his plays by a more moderate character, who contrasts with the hero (e.g. Odysseus in *Ajax*, Chrysothemis in *Electra*).

The common features of the Sophoclean hero have been discussed by Bernard Knox in *The Heroic Temper*, who points out the distinctive language which they use (pp. 10-44). Most of these features are exemplified by Electra. She resolves to act, expressing herself decisively with future tenses: 'I will not cease from my laments' (103), 'I will not live inside in future' (818), 'I will not let the deed come to nothing' (1020). Her resolve is tested by emotional appeals from Chrysothemis, to which she refers dismissively as 'reproofs' (343, 595, 1025). Chrysothemis appeals to reason (384, 1048, 1056), but Electra refuses either to learn (330, 370, 395, 889, 1032) or to yield (361, 396, 1014). She hates even those who would help her (367, 1027, 1033). There are repeated references to her anger (176, 218-22, 331, 369, 1011). She is accused of foolishness and lack of sense (398, 1013, 1016), and of being bold and rash (626, 995, 1446). She is immoderate and excessive (140, 155, 236), and refuses to be changed by time (330, 1013, 1030). She cannot endure the life of a slave (264, 814, 970, 1192). When she says ironically to Aegisthus 'I have acquired sense in time, so as to comply with those who are more powerful' (1464-5), she is pretending to do what the Sophoclean hero never does. She curses her enemies (112-16), and the thought of their triumphant laughter is unendurable (807, 1153). Her uncompromising nature means that she must act and suffer alone (119, 1019, 1074). There is no place for her on earth, and she is not only prepared to accept death but positively longs for it (820-2, 1078-80, 1165-70).

Knox stresses that Sophocles' heroes are not stereotypical or lacking in individuality. He remarks on 'that irreducible center of particularity, of uniqueness, which in the last analysis ... is the only source of the heroic will to defy the world' (p. 37). A passionate and uncompromising subjectivity is one of the most notable features of these characters. Knox observes, 'Electra, the most self-analytical of all the Sophoclean heroes, is fully aware of her uniqueness; she can feel shame at the outrageous conduct to which it sometimes drives her ..., but also a fierce pride in her independence of spirit' (p. 38).

Electra's lamentation

Electra appears first alone, as she comes out of the palace and delivers a monody, or solo song. She addresses the light and the air, which have witnessed so much lamentation and breast-beating by her in the past. She will not stop lamenting as long as she sees the stars and the light of day. Sophocles conveys a strong sense of the endless repetition of her laments and of her confrontations with those who would make her discontinue them (cf. 88-9, 255, 372-3, 552-3). She is compared three times to 'the nightingale who killed her child' (107; cf. 147-9, 1077). This is an allusion to the myth of Procne. She killed her son Itys, and served him up to her husband Tereus to eat, in revenge for the latter's rape and mutilation of her sister Philomela. Tereus pursued the sisters, but the gods turned all three into birds. Procne is the nightingale, with her song 'Itys! Itys!'. Her eternal nature is determined by lamentation. Electra also admires Niobe, who has been turned to stone and weeps perpetually for her children (150-2). Agamemnon was killed 'shamefully' (102, 206, 486), 'pitifully' (100, 102, 145, 193-4), and 'unjustly' (113). Electra identifies herself with him as 'wretched' (77, 80, 94) and 'betrayed' (126, 208). She concludes the monody by calling on the gods to avenge his murder and to send Orestes to her.

The chorus offers a series of consolatory commonplaces

which prompts Electra to emphasize the abnormality of her situation. They can be paraphrased as follows: 'Why do you always lament insatiably for the long-dead Agamemnon? Everyone must go to Hades, and you will not bring him back by lamenting. You will only make things worse for yourself. You are not the only person to suffer bereavement, and your siblings react less extravagantly. The gods are not heedless. You are only making more trouble for yourself.' One of the key words which characterizes her behaviour is 'always' (122, 141, 148, 165, 218). Another is the prefix *hyper-*, denoting excess in Greek as in English (176-7, 217). John Gould observes: 'To Electra's sense of the ordered naturalness of her unceasing grief, the chorus opposes a different but equally coherent sense of a natural order, one to which loss is native, in which time will bring restoral and to which Electra's grief is a senseless, even sacrilegious, challenge' (p. 95).

Electra begins her reply by reiterating that she will not stop lamenting Agamemnon (132-3). She condemns the child who could forget a parent's piteous death, and insists that Procne and Niobe suit her character better (145-52). Her suffering is extreme: 'I bear an endless fate of sorrows, always going my sad way wet with tears, without husband and children' (164-8). Electra's name was believed to mean 'unmarried', and this is a distinctive element of her suffering (cf. 187-8, 961-2).[5] She wears squalid clothes and is treated as a slave (189-92; cf. 264-5, 597-600, 814-15, 1192-6), a motif which appeared already at Aeschylus, *Libation Bearers* 135. She wastes away (187, 283, 835, 1181), and repeatedly complains that she is 'destroyed' (208, 304, 674, 677, 808, 830).

Electra gradually finds words for the moral principles which govern her behaviour. She has the social awareness to express gratitude for the chorus' kind words (129-36), and has a strong sense of being deprived of her proper social status (187-92). She understands that her behaviour is unusual: 'I have been forced by terrible circumstances to do terrible things; I know it well, my passion does not escape me. But even in these terrible circumstances I will not restrain my desperate laments, while life is in me. Who, dear friends, who that thinks rightly, could expect me to listen to any word of consolation? Leave me, leave me, my comforters' (221-9). She defends her behaviour by the standard of what 'a right-thinking person' would believe. She then expresses the idea that it cannot be honourable (*kalos*) to neglect the dead, and that if such neglect is anywhere innate in humans then she would not wish to be honoured by them (237-9). She is thus constantly aware of an idealized social sanction, and does not merely follow wilful personal predilections. She finally justifies herself by the central moral terms of shame (*aidôs*) and piety, which will vanish from the earth if the dead are to be 'dust and nothingness' and murderers are not punished (245-50).

Richard Seaford has given an interesting account of Electra's lamentation in terms of anthropology.[6] He points out that death is seen in many communities as a transitional process which is marked by rites of passage. Mourners participate in the state of the recently deceased by withdrawing from the community, and by eating and dressing differently from the living. After a period of time (e.g. a month), the deceased is assumed to be fully incorporated into the world of the dead, and the mourners are reintegrated into the society of the living. Seaford observes that Agamemnon is not fully incorporated into the world of the dead because he has not received a funeral, and Clytemnestra even celebrates his death with a monthly festival (278-81). Electra, for her part, has no acceptable society to rejoin. She is thus anomalously trapped in a condition of perpetual mourning from which she cannot emerge. She complains that her wretched condition is inflicted by her enemies, but it is also appropriate to a mourner. Her continued mourning is a ritual expression of the disorder in her family, and a refusal to accept the normality of the present state of affairs. Electra also sees her lamentation as a form of revenge, in that it harasses and intimidates Clytemnestra (349-50, 355, 556-7, 654). Clytemnestra admits as much, both in her threat to incarcerate Electra (379-82) and in what she says when she believes that Orestes is dead (783-7).

Electra now makes a speech which both recapitulates and

justifies her lamentation in the preceding lyrics (254-309). She begins: 'I am ashamed, women, if you think that I grieve too much with my many laments; but forgive me, since a hard compulsion forces me to do this' (254-7). The concept of shame is central to the assessment of Electra's behaviour, both by herself and others. 'Shame' is in fact an inadequate rendering of a concept expressed by a number of related words in Greek, the main one of which is *aidôs*. Robert Parker helpfully defines *aidôs* as 'self-restraint expressed through respect for recognized values'.[7] *Aidôs* also developed a retrospective sense, referring to shame at having done wrong. *Aidôs* is essentially a matter of regard for other people and how things appear to them, but it must be stressed that it is not merely servile deference to a purely external sanction. Bernard Williams has argued that *aidôs* involves respect for an other who is internalized, and to whose opinion one assents. In Homer's *Iliad*, Hector worries about possible criticism by someone 'worse' than himself (22.106), but only because he accepts that the criticisms would be true. There is no reason to suppose that he would be incapable of ignoring unfair criticism by someone whom he despised. Williams stresses, however, that the essentially other-directed nature of *aidôs* should not be overlooked. 'The internalised other is indeed abstracted and generalised and idealised, but he is potentially somebody rather than nobody, and somebody other than me.'[8] This distinguishes *aidôs* from guilt.

Electra has argued that *aidôs* requires that the murdered Agamemnon should be mourned (245-50). On the other hand, her persistent public lamentation is a violation of the norms of female behaviour, and thus also shows a lack of *aidôs*. Aegisthus previously kept her inside so that she would not 'shame her family (*philoi*)' (518). Christopher Gill has argued that Sophocles' heroes do not adopt 'ethical individualism' (as expressed e.g. by Nietzsche or Sartre), but that they 'appeal (in their second-order reasoning) to ethical principles which they regard as basic to their society'.[9] Electra thus proceeds immediately to consider the imaginary norm of how a 'noble' woman would behave in the circumstances in which she finds herself

(257). Her recognition of the fact that her behaviour is abnormal seems itself to show *aidôs*. This self-awareness is a key aspect of her character (cf. 131, 221-9, 307-9, 612-21).

Electra introduces two more ethical principles in the final three lines of her speech: 'In such conditions, my friends, one cannot be *sôphrôn* or pious; but in bad circumstances it is necessary that one's behaviour should also be bad' (307-9). These lines allude to Aeschylus' *Libation Bearers*, where Electra prays to be more *sôphrôn* and pious than Clytemnestra (140-1). The Sophoclean hero tends not to be *sôphrôn*, but it is striking that Electra is so intensely aware of the reasons which prevent her from being so. 'Piety' here refers to the respect that is due to parents, which Electra cannot maintain towards Clytemnestra. This was closely associated with piety towards the gods, and Electra will indeed be praised by the chorus for her 'piety towards Zeus' (1097) in the specific context of her mourning for Agamemnon (cf. 464, 968). She is again in a quandary, since she cannot show appropriate piety to both parents.

Electra and Chrysothemis I

Electra's character is further defined in her two scenes with Chrysothemis. The chorus' sympathetic criticisms in the *parodos* gave her the opportunity to justify her behaviour. Chrysothemis' criticisms are more sharply focussed, in that they come from an individual rather than a group, and from one who has herself made a distinctly different choice about how to behave.

There is a conflict between Electra's understanding of *sôphrosunê* and Chrysothemis' more conventional views about female behaviour. Electra alleges that if Chrysothemis were *sôphrôn* she would not want the privileges which she gains from supporting her mother and betraying her father (363-8). The chorus later tells Chrysothemis that she would be *sôphrôn* if she followed Electra's suggestion about replacing Clytemnestra's offerings to Agamemnon with different ones of their own (465).

More often, the sisters conduct their discussion in the slightly more general terms of 'good sense' (one Greek word for this, *phronein*, is cognate with *sôphrôn*). Chrysothemis repeatedly accuses Electra of lacking good sense, meaning that her actions are disadvantageous to her (384, 394, 398, 992-3, 1038, 1055-6). The terminology reappears in Electra's scene with Clytemnestra (529, 550-1). She herself refuses 'to give the impression of doing something, while actually doing no harm to our enemies' (336). She keeps coming back to the idea that they lack the strength to resist effectively (333, 348, 946, 998, 1014). Electra, by contrast, challenges her to choose between being 'foolish' (i.e. behaving as she, Electra, is doing) and showing 'good sense' and betraying her *philoi* (345-6). Electra says that she would be 'empty of sense' if she were to be as subservient as Chrysothemis (403). Later she says 'I envy you your good sense, but hate you for your cowardice' (1027). She is confident that public opinion will support her (366), and Chrysothemis herself accepts that her 'good sense' is prudent rather than just (338-9, 1041-2).

Electra and Clytemnestra

The formal features of Electra's agon with Clytemnestra were discussed in Chapter 3, which also included some comments on Clytemnestra's speech. The present section will look a little more closely at Electra's speech, and at her contribution to the dialogue which follows the two main speeches. Scholars' views of Electra's part in this scene reflect their interpretations of the play as a whole. Those with an 'affirmative' view of the play think that she comprehensively refutes Clytemnestra (e.g. Burton, p. 203; March, pp. 176-9), while those with a darker view of it stress the corruption of Electra's character and the similarities which emerge between the two women (e.g. Friis Johansen, pp. 15-20; Blundell, pp. 161-72).

In the first section of her speech (558-62), Electra argues that Clytemnestra's motive for killing Agamemnon was adultery, and not (as she alleged) revenge for the sacrifice of Iphigenia.

This question was raised by Pindar, and explored at length in Aeschylus' *Oresteia* (see Chapter 2). Electra has no doubt about the answer.

The second section of Electra's speech (563-76) is especially interesting for the account which it gives of the reasons for Artemis' anger: 'My father, as I have heard, was sporting in the grove of the goddess when his footfall disturbed a dappled and antlered stag; and on killing it he happened to utter a boastful word' (566-9). Electra follows the *Cypria* version, which differs from Aeschylus' version where Artemis is angry at an omen which symbolizes Agamemnon's destruction of innocent life (*Agamemnon* 134-8). Electra adds a crucial detail to the *Cypria* version when she says that Artemis not only prevented the Greeks from sailing to Troy but also prevented them from going home. Agamemnon was thus unable to save Iphigenia by renouncing the war, and was obliged to sacrifice her if the Greeks were not to remain at Aulis for ever. A. Maria van Erp Taalman Kip observes: 'This considerably lessens his guilt, while Clytaemnestra is largely deprived of what might have been a righteous motive for her deed ... But is what Electra says true? Or, to be more precise: are the audience meant to accept her information as true?'[10] This is certainly a valid question. Athenian citizens were accustomed to assessing arguments in the assembly and in the courts, and would no doubt have responded in somewhat similar fashion to argumentative speeches in the theatre. This would have been especially the case with agon scenes, with their pronounced forensic flavour. These agon scenes often contain assertions which cannot be checked, but that does not mean that we should not reflect on their plausibility.

Van Erp Taalman Kip herself argues that there is no reason to disbelieve what Electra says: 'Electra's account is nowhere contradicted. Apparently we are meant to believe it and to accept its implications.'[11] It is indeed true that Clytemnestra does not contradict it, but her sceptical and secular account of the sacrifice has already implied the rejection of human access to divine involvement of the kind alleged by Electra (534-48). In

Sophocles, the actions and motives of the gods are normally inaccessible to mortals. Neoptolemus may know the divine background to Philoctetes' injury from the prophet Helenus (*Philoctetes* 1326-42), but Philoctetes himself had regarded it as an accident (267, 632). Electra says 'as I hear' (566), but would have carried more conviction if she had named her source (e.g. the prophet Calchas). This vagueness about the source of her information contrasts with the decorative detail which she supplies, especially the epic colouring of 'a dappled and antlered stag' (568; cf. Homer, *Iliad* 3.24). She then says that Agamemnon 'happened to utter a boastful word' (569), concealing with euphemistic language the details – invariable in this version of the story – of his offence. Finally, there is her unparalleled, and somewhat improbable, claim that Agamemnon could not even disband the army without sacrificing Iphigenia (contrast Aeschylus, *Agamemnon* 212-13 and Euripides, *Iphigenia at Aulis* 94-6).

Sophocles thus gives us several reasons to question Electra's argument in this section, even if much remains undecided. The nuances of Agamemnon's guilt are treated at length in some versions of the story, but here the focus is more on Electra's view of him. She seems to be embroidering some details and suppressing others, and the overall effect is to give the most favourable account of Agamemnon.

The third section of Electra's speech has also been much debated (577-84). She argues that even if Agamemnon were guilty, that would not have been a reason for Clytemnestra to kill him. 'Take care that in laying down this law for mortals you do not lay down pain and regret for yourself. For if we are to take a life for a life, you would be the first to die, if you were to get what you deserve' (580-3). Many critics have argued that these lines have an ironic relevance to the murders which Orestes and Electra will soon commit (e.g. Winnington-Ingram, p. 221; Blundell, p. 168). Other scholars have objected that Electra's words have a purely localized significance, and that we should not pursue their implications beyond the immediate argumentative context (e.g. March, note on lines 580-3). This objection places arbitrary limitations on the significance of tragic rhetoric, and overlooks suggestions elsewhere in the play that it is Electra's understanding of events that is limited. A more sophisticated objection to an ironic reading of these lines is that they are a threat, rather than a justification of Electra's revenge. Her real motive is justice, while Orestes has been commanded by Apollo. Clytemnestra herself also appealed to justice, however, and did not simply rely on the *lex talionis* (the principle that the punishment should resemble the offence).

Electra goes on to criticize Clytemnestra for living with Agamemnon's murderer (584-94) and maltreating her children (595-605). The conclusion of her speech is especially interesting. She challenges Clytemnestra to say of her what she will, 'denounce me to all the world, if you like, for being bad or loud-mouthed or full of shamelessness; for if it is in my nature to behave like this then perhaps I am no unworthy child of yours' (606-9). Clytemnestra responds by accusing Electra of shamelessness and *hybris* (wanton violence or injustice, contempt for another person's rights). Electra replies: 'Be sure that I do feel shame for these things, even if it does not look like that to you. I understand that my behaviour is unseemly and contrary to my real nature, but it is your hostility and your actions which force me to act in this way; for shameful [*aischros*] behaviour is taught by shameful deeds' (616-21). This recapitulates her earlier statement to the chorus that she is forced into shameful behaviour. Electra and Clytemnestra repeatedly accuse each other of *hybris* (271, 293, 522-3, 613, 790, 794).

Holger Friis Johansen has given an eloquent psychological account of Electra's predicament:

> Electra is the daughter of Agamemnon; but she is also, whether she likes it or not, the daughter of Clytemnestra. She has a part of her mother in herself, and living with her has caused precisely this part to become fully developed (p. 17).

5. Electra

Friis Johansen contrasts Electra with other Sophoclean heroes such as Ajax, Antigone, and Oedipus:

> They sacrifice life or happiness, but Electra sacrifices her character. Even before the arrival of Orestes she has for many years prepared herself in her mother's school for the role of avenger of her mother. In order to accomplish the act of revenge with Orestes, she must in a sense make herself similar to her opponent, which is well-nigh incompatible with the nature of a Sophoclean hero, and which fills her with shame and disgust; for she remains a heroine throughout – otherwise, we should just have a commonplace melodrama before us rather than a tragedy (p. 31).

Thomas Szlezák has argued, by contrast, that it is precisely Electra's shame that distinguishes her from Clytemnestra (254, 616). She is aware that she is being forced to act in a way that is out of keeping with the traditional social role of a young woman, while Clytemnestra is unrepentant (549-51).

> But it is not primarily the horrified dismay at her own obstinacy that separates the daughter from her mother, but rather where their obstinacy leads the two women: the mother to continuing her immoral marriage to her accomplice in the murder ... as well as to ill-treating her legitimate children and depriving them of their rights (585-94, 1195-6), the daughter on the other hand to frankly calling a crime a crime (pp. 12-13).

Szlezák insists that Electra's words 'shameful behaviour is taught by shameful deeds' (621) are a bitterly sarcastic retort rather than an objective statement which could be used as the cornerstone of an interpretation of her character. Clytemnestra resorts to criticism of Electra's disrespect to her when she has lost the debate over justice (613-14). Electra is sensitive to this criticism, although she feels compelled to behave as she does

(616-20). She constantly aspires to the nobler virtues (236-50, 257, 968-89, 1074-97).

There is something to be said for both these positions, which are perhaps not as far apart as they may seem. Szlezák is right that Electra's remarks need to be taken in context, and that she is not nearly as bad as Clytemnestra. On the other hand, her self-awareness does not alter the reality of what her predicament has done to her, and her aspirations towards nobler virtues do not mean that she achieves them. Friis Johansen is correct to insist that she retains her heroic status, and that she is not merely corrupted. It is indeed typically tragic that someone should be fully aware of what is wrong with their behaviour, but be unable (for internal or external reasons) to change it.

Electra and Chrysothemis II

Electra is convinced by the Paedagogus' messenger speech that Orestes is dead, and now proposes to Chrysothemis that the two of them together should kill Aegisthus. She argues that their only prospects now are of growing old unmarried, lamenting the loss of their father's wealth. If they succeed in killing Aegisthus, then they will not only have acted piously towards Agamemnon but will be rewarded by freedom and marriage. Electra imagines what will be said about them in the city (975-85):

> What citizen or foreigner will not greet us with praise when he sees us: 'Look at these sisters, friends, who saved their father's house, and did not spare their lives in taking vengeance on their enemies. All should love them, all should revere them, all should honour them at feasts and at gatherings in the city for their courage.' Such things will be said about us by everyone, so that in life and death our fame [*kleos*] will never die.

Electra locates her project in a tradition of heroism which goes back at least to Homer, where fame is what the warrior hopes to win. Achilles chose a short life with 'immortal fame' above a long and inglorious life (*Iliad* 9.410-16). Orestes won 'fame among everyone' for killing Aegisthus (*Odyssey* 1.298-9). Warriors imagine what will be said about them. Sarpedon hopes that his Lycian subjects will say that their kings are 'not inglorious', and that their heroism shows that they deserve the honours and rewards which they receive (*Iliad* 12.310-28). Hector quotes imaginary compliments about his prowess, and adds the formulaic phrase 'my fame will never die' (*Iliad* 7.87-91). The language of heroism was adapted to the more collective ethos of democratic Athens. Thucydides reports Pericles as saying in his funeral speech over the Athenian war dead in 431/0 BC: 'They sacrificed their lives for Athens, and gained for themselves praises which never grow old, the most splendid of graves – not the one in which their bodies are laid, but where their glory is always remembered' (2.43.2). Electra's phrase 'did not spare their lives' (980) is common in such contexts. Pericles goes on to speak of warriors being 'unsparing' of their lives (2.43.5), and the same word is used by Lysias (2.25) in the early fourth century in his praise of the Athenian dead at Marathon.

Electra is not the only female character in tragedy to express herself in terms of the heroic ethos. Antigone is partly motivated by the fame (*kleos*) which she will gain from burying her brother (*Antigone* 502-5), and she takes the typically heroic view that it would be a fine (*kalos*) thing to die in the process of doing such a deed (*Antigone* 72, 96-7). Haemon reports the view of the Thebans that she has done a 'most glorious deed' for which she deserves 'honour' (*Antigone* 692-700). Bernard Knox has demonstrated in detail how Euripides' Medea is presented in distinctively heroic terms.[12] Electra's project may seem fantastic, but there are plenty of examples in tragedy and myth of women taking violent revenge on men (e.g. in Euripides' *Medea* and *Hecuba*).

Electra's revenge plan may not be impracticable, but we know that it is deluded and superfluous now that Orestes has returned. This makes her heroism difficult to assess. Her behaviour in the earlier part of the play may be the response of an extreme individual to an extreme situation, but it is at least grounded in a correct understanding of her circumstances. Her false belief that Orestes is dead leads to an increasing disjunction between her subjective apprehension of events and their true nature. This is clear in her revenge proposal here, and also in her lament over the urn. The lament is one of the most powerful and subjectively intense speeches in all Greek tragedy, but the urn is empty and the living Orestes is standing beside her.

Another problem is that Electra proposes to kill only Aegisthus, as 'our father's murderer' (955-7). Her later reference to 'enemies' (979) may include Clytemnestra, but could also be a generalizing plural referring only to Aegisthus. Earlier in the play, Electra has regularly spoken of Clytemnestra as being jointly responsible for the murder of Agamemnon (97-9, 206, 587-8), and as being equally deserving of punishment (603-5). A wide range of explanations has been given of Electra's failure to mention her here. Some scholars think that she is deliberately deceiving Chrysothemis by omitting an aspect of the proposal from which she might be expected to recoil. Others argue that Electra deceives herself by presenting the revenge in an heroic light and failing to consider the more problematic matricide. A third school of thought is that it is Sophocles who is suppressing the problem of matricide and focussing on Electra's heroism in planning to kill the more dangerous enemy (for details of the scholars who have held these views, see MacLeod, p. 141 n. 7; March, note on lines 955-7). It is evident that this debate is a microcosm of the conflicting views of the play as a whole. There is little or no explicit discussion anywhere in the play of possible problems with the matricide. Electra's revenge plan is only one example of this.

Electra's revenge

Orestes is quite dispassionate about the revenge. He prays to be restored to his ancestral house, of which he is 'a just cleanser sent by the gods' (69-72), he wants 'to stop our enemies laughing' (1295), and he says that wrongdoers should be killed outright (1505-7). He wants to get on with the job as quickly and efficiently as possible (73-6, 1288-95, 1372-5, 1491-1502). This contrasts strikingly with Electra's passionate hatred of the usurpers.

Sophocles emphasizes Electra's passion for revenge on two occasions while the murders are being carried out. Clytemnestra cries out from inside the palace that she has been struck, and Electra's response is to encourage Orestes: 'Strike, if you have the strength, for a second time!' (1415). This echoes the murder of Agamemnon in Aeschylus' *Agamemnon* (1343-6). T.C.W. Stinton writes: 'the dramatic point of the close recall of Aeschylus' scene is to show the murderess getting precisely what she gave' (p. 474). Electra's outburst is nonetheless revealing. David Seale points out that it is she who replies to Clytemnestra's appeal to Orestes for pity, and she who orders him to strike again: 'The myth requires that Orestes commit the matricide but Electra appears mentally, if not physically, to appropriate the act by the violence of the language with which she wills it' (p. 75). This remarkable piece of stagecraft confirms the distinction between Electra's yearning for revenge and Orestes' dispassionate execution of it. Most commentators, even those who believe that the revenge is just, have been repelled by the savagery of her words here. Some, however, feel that Electra's outburst is justified in terms of Clytemnestra's wickedness, the emotional intensity of the moment, or uninhibited Greek views of the pleasures of revenge (e.g. March, note on lines 1415-16).

Electra also replies to an appeal to Orestes by Aegisthus: 'No, kill him at once, and give his corpse to the appropriate buriers' (1487-8). Jebb comments that these 'buriers' are dogs and birds. This generally accepted identification is confirmed by the allusion to Nestor's account in Homer of what Menelaus would have done to Aegisthus: 'dogs and birds would have devoured him as he lay on the plain outside the city' (*Odyssey* 3.259-60). The problem is that, while this treatment is routinely meted out to the corpses of enemy warriors in Homer, it is regarded as impious elsewhere in Sophocles (*Ajax, Antigone*). Electra's lan-

93

guage is, however, vague and contemptuous. There is no hint of any systematic attempt to deny burial to Aegisthus, but also no gesture towards piety. She remains intensely vindictive to the end.

Scholars who believe in the justice of the revenge in *Electra* draw support from the widely accepted principle in Greek ethics of helping *philoi* and harming enemies (e.g. Stevens, p. 119). A classic exposition of this view is in Book 1 of Plato's *Republic*, where Socrates elucidates Polemarchus' definition of justice from his support of a saying of Simonides that it is just to give each person their due: 'So Simonides says that justice is to benefit one's *philoi* and harm one's enemies?' (332d). There can indeed be no doubt that this was a fundamental principle of Greek ethics, but it is often problematic in tragedy. Jenny March illustrates it by quoting, as an example of 'accepted Greek morality', the words of Medea (Euripides, *Medea* 807-10): 'Let no one think me contemptible, or weak, or easy-going. No, quite the opposite, harsh to enemies and kindly to friends [*philoi*]. Such people live a life of greatest glory' (p. 19). These lines actually conclude a speech, delivered by a barbarian woman, in which she proposes to kill her own children. The speaker is not Greek, and her proposal is not morally acceptable to the chorus.

Revenge was undoubtedly a temptation and a pleasure for fifth-century Athenian citizens, but it was also a temptation which they needed in some measure to resist. No doubt they had many of the attitudes and impulses which have been grouped by anthropologists under the heading 'Mediterranean values', including an intense concern for their honour and the urge to immediate and violent retaliation for any slight on it.[13] Such values inevitably conflicted with the requirement in Athens to pursue grievances through the courts, and in particular to refrain from resorting to physical violence.[14] Homicide courts are not, of course, a regular feature of the heroic world in which *Electra* is set, and it is a typically Euripidean paradox when Tyndareus says that Orestes should have prosecuted Clytemnestra (Euripides, *Orestes* 492-506). Orestes may indeed have been obliged to accomplish revenge by his own hand, but that does not mean that the 'harm enemies' principle can straightforwardly justify the violence which this involves. This is especially the case when revenge involves killing his mother. Mary Whitlock Blundell points to the disruption of natural relationships between *philoi* in *Electra*: 'The murders of Iphigeneia and Agamemnon have created two warring groups of *philoi*, cutting across the normal lines of family solidarity' (p. 151).

It is a remarkable feature of Greek tragedy that many of the most vindictive characters are women. This is especially the case in the plays of Euripides, where we find not only Electra (*Electra*), but also Medea (*Medea*), Alcmena (*Children of Heracles*), Phaedra (*Hippolytus*), Hermione (*Andromache*), Hecuba (*Hecuba*), Iphigenia (*Iphigenia among the Taurians*), and Creusa (*Ion*). Orestes kills Clytemnestra as a matter of duty in all three tragedians, and with the utmost reluctance in Aeschylus and Euripides. It is only the mad, post-matricide Orestes who is passionately vindictive (*Andromache*, *Orestes*). Vindictive men are rarely far from insanity. Ajax (Sophocles, *Ajax*) and Heracles (Euripides, *Heracles*) both go mad in the process of taking revenge. Cold-hearted cruelty and devious political calculation may be gendered as male, but vindictiveness is distinctively female.

This is not to say that the tragedians were making the point that real women behaved in this way. Violent acts of revenge in real life were no doubt performed in the overwhelming majority of cases by men, but female characters in tragedy serve a wider function than representing actual women (see Chapter 1 n. 9). The dichotomy between male and female is deeply ingrained in human thought, and serves as a useful tool to categorize a range of characteristics which are not in reality the exclusive preserve of one sex or the other. Roger Just thus offers a list of opposing masculine and feminine traits in (male) Athenian thought:

men are strong, women are weak; men are brave, women are fearful; men are magnanimous, women are vindictive;

men are reserved, women are loquacious; men are rational, women are irrational; men are self-controlled, women are self-indulgent – and so forth …. In any society the concept of masculinity and femininity are defined by mutual opposition and women tend to be portrayed as what men, ideally, are not.[15]

Female characters in tragedy can thus represent all that is antisocial and disruptive, without necessarily implying that real women behaved in such an extreme way. Revenge is one of those powerful human impulses which the Athenian male citizen must either suppress altogether or channel through orderly social structures. The unsocialized impulse to retaliate is projected in drama onto women, along with a wide range of other antisocial emotions and activities. None of this is to deny that Electra is in some respects a 'woman' who is liable to assessment by the ethical principles applicable to women, as discussed above. Femininity would lose its shape as a concept if it were not grounded in a dramatically convincing portrayal of actual women. Nonetheless, it is striking that it is Electra rather than Orestes who has a passion for revenge. The contrast between male and female attitudes to revenge is nowhere clearer than in *Electra*.

Conclusion

Electra is as complex a character as there is in the whole of Greek tragedy. She begins by expressing an acute sense of her predicament as the daughter of a king. The norms of female behaviour prescribe restraint (*sôphrosunê*), but the duty to lament her murdered father requires her to make an extreme and prolonged demonstration of grief. In the earlier part of the play, at least, this seems to be an heroic and self-sacrificing response to a tragic dilemma. She has the unrelenting courage and obstinacy of the Sophoclean hero, and refuses to heed any advice to compromise with the usurpers. She is intensely aware of the ethical sacrifices this entails.

5. Electra

Sophocles' heroes invariably repel too comfortable an identification with their passionate subjectivity. Doubts start to surface about the reliability of Electra's view of Agamemnon in her debate with Clytemnestra. Sophocles is not so much interested in Agamemnon's behaviour in itself as in Electra's determination to justify it at all costs. Her belief after the Paedagogus' messenger speech that Orestes is dead means that her behaviour for the next 450 lines is founded on delusion. This sequence includes her rejection of Chrysothemis' announcement that Orestes has returned, her plan to kill Aegisthus, and her lament over the urn. Her heroism and grief are now purely subjective, and not rooted in the understanding of her situation that she had earlier. Sophocles draws the audience into identifying with her emotions, while at the same time alienating it from them. Her passion for revenge is similarly ambiguous, but any interpretation of this will depend on one's view of the justice of the matricide itself.

6

Matricide

The justice of the matricide in *Electra* is one of the most vigorously debated issues in all Greek tragedy. Some scholars adopt an 'affirmative' view that the matricide is just, and that Orestes and Electra are therefore right not to be troubled by it. Others take an 'ironic' view, that the play implies doubts about the justice of the matricide. A compromise interpretation is that the matricide may be just, but that it is nevertheless an ugly and degrading act. Finally, there are critics who regard the character of Electra as being the main subject of the play, and put less emphasis on the moral issues of the matricide. These last two interpretations were discussed in Chapter 5, and the focus in the present chapter will be the issue of the matricide itself.

The affirmative interpretation

Jebb thought that 'Sophocles regards the vengeance as a deed of unalloyed merit, which brings the troubles of the house to an end' (pp. xxxix-xl). He observed that Orestes has no qualms about the matricide: 'he neither shrinks from it in prospect, nor feels the slightest uneasiness when it has been accomplished. From first to last, his confidence is as cheerful as the morning sunshine in which the action commences' (p. xl). He argued that Sophocles treated the revenge in 'epic' terms as a glorious feat, suppressing any 'tragic' concerns about the matricide. 'Sophocles seems to say to his audience, "I give you, modified for drama, the story that Homer tells; put yourselves at the Homeric stand-point; regard the act of Orestes under the light in which the *Odyssey* presents it" ' (p. xli). Nothing could be further from Aeschylus' and Euripides' treatments of the story, where the matricide is highly problematic and Orestes is subsequently pursued by the Furies. It is an argument in favour of the affirmative view of the play that Orestes and Electra have no doubts about the justice of the revenge either before or after the murders, and that both Chrysothemis and the chorus are generally in agreement with them about it. The possibility that the matricide may be problematic is not considered by anyone. The gods take a similar attitude. Apollo has ordered the revenge, and there are at least hints that other gods support it. Electra's prayers (110-20, 1376-83) seem to be answered, while Clytemnestra's prayer (634-59) is not. The Furies do not appear at the end, and there is no explicit indication that Orestes will be pursued by them.

More recent supporters of the affirmative interpretation of the play argue that Sophocles does not merely avoid the moral problems of the matricide (as Jebb thought), but that he actually shows it to be just. Jenny March writes: 'we should look at the play in the light of fifth-century beliefs, where moral excellence lay in doing not only good to one's friends [*philoi*], but harm to one's enemies; where repaying evil for evil as well as good for good was accepted Greek morality' (p. 19). It was argued in Chapter 5 that there were limits to the applicability of this principle in fifth-century Athens, especially when violence was involved. Furthermore, the principle is obviously difficult to apply in *Electra*, where Clytemnestra both is and is not a *philos* of Orestes. Thomas Szlezák thinks that this view of revenge has wrongly been rejected because it is unacceptable to modern moral feeling: 'Has Sophocles merely got the bleak message to convey to us, that violence can only be overcome by violence?' (p. 2). Szlezák believes that this is indeed the message of the play.

Another argument for the affirmative view is that Sophocles has made Clytemnestra so bad that we need not be troubled by her murder. Not all of the allegations against her are equally strong, but there can be no doubt that she is worse in Sophocles than in Aeschylus or Euripides. She not only killed Agamemnon but mutilated his corpse, the rite of *maschalismos* designed to disable the spirit of the dead man from taking revenge (444-6; cf. Aeschylus, *Libation Bearers* 439). She has no regrets for what she has done (549-51), and even has a monthly celebration of the day of Agamemnon's death (277-81). Electra alleges that she would have killed Orestes if he had not been sent away (296-7, 601, 1131-5; cf. 11, 1348-52). Clytemnestra expresses grief for his death (766-72), although it has been suggested that she prayed for it shortly before (637-59), and Electra doubts her sincerity (804-7, 929). She treats Electra badly, and has lost her claim to the title 'mother' (273-4, 597-8, 1154, 1194). There are many references to her sexual offences (97, 114, 197, 492-4, 561-2, 587-9).

Finally, there are a number of features of Sophocles' handling of the action which seem calculated to suppress the problem of the matricide. P.T. Stevens writes: 'the act of matricide was an essential part of the story and was deeply repugnant, if anyone paused to think about it; but it is significant that Sophocles exercises his skill in discouraging his audience from dwelling on it' (p. 117). Revenge on Agamemnon's murderers is mentioned fairly frequently, but only in rather vague and general language. There is nothing remotely comparable to the Euripidean Electra's 'May I die once I have shed my mother's blood in vengeance!' (Euripides, *Electra* 281; cf. 647). Electra focusses at crucial moments on Aegisthus rather than on Clytemnestra (e.g. 266-70, 956-7). Orestes does not meet Clytemnestra on stage before the murder (as in Aeschylus), or even see her approaching from a distance (as in Euripides). The order of the murders is changed, with the arrival of Aegisthus cutting short any reflection on the murder of Clytemnestra. One explanation of this is that Sophocles wants to conclude the play with the less problematic of the two murders. The recognition of Orestes and Electra is delayed to the latest possible moment. It occurs in Sophocles at line 1224 (out of 1510), in contrast to line 233 (out of 1076) in Aeschylus and line 577 (out of 1358) in Euripides. The murders seem merely to be an appendage to the climactic reunion of brother and sister. Clytemnestra's dream stresses the re-establishment of legitimate authority in Mycenae (417-23), rather than (as in Aeschylus) the murder of a mother by her son.

The ironic interpretation

The view that Sophocles condemns the matricide was proposed by J.T. Sheppard in three articles published between 1918 and 1927.[1] His main argument was that Orestes asked the Delphic oracle *how* he should take revenge rather than *whether* he should take it (32-7), begging the question of whether he should take revenge at all. Apollo's answer is in a tradition of oracular responses which lead on to destruction those who approach it with evil intentions and tendentious questions. This interpretation of the oracle was taken up by J.H. Kells in his edition, but is not now generally accepted. The text implies that Apollo regarded the revenge as 'just' (37), and Sophocles gives no hint that Orestes misinterpreted the god's meaning. Sheppard reinforced his view with other points, and his ironic interpretation has been developed with greater scope and subtlety by later scholars.

The strongest argument in favour of the ironic interpretation is that matricide is such an inherently problematic act that the failure of anyone in the play to address that fact is inevitably significant. Such an act may conceivably be justifiable in the most extreme circumstances, but it is difficult to see how it could be treated as unproblematic in any serious literature that is not self-consciously absurdist. Electra may be sure of the justice of the revenge, but she is also comprehensively deluded for much of the play. She eventually discovers the truth about Orestes' return, but Sophocles has not allowed us to identify too closely with her passionate conviction. A somewhat more moderate view (not his own) is summarized by Winnington-Ingram as follows: 'Sophocles might be saying ... "I know that matricide is a terrible thing, but I have made this mother so utterly bad that, on a choice of evils, the children were justified in killing her ..." ' (p. 225). In Aeschylus' *Oresteia*, Orestes is, in the end, acquitted. The problem in *Electra* is that there is no hint anywhere of 'a choice of evils', or indeed of any awareness on the part of the avengers that there are anything other than practical obstacles to killing Clytemnestra. The affirmative interpretation would be stronger if the moral problem of matricide were not so completely ignored by the avengers.

The problematic nature of matricide is not just a matter of common moral feelings, but was a main theme of Aeschylus' *Oresteia*, where it is the centre of attention for nearly a thousand lines of the trilogy. It was argued in Chapter 2 that the *Oresteia* looms large in the background to *Electra*. If this is so, then the possibility that the matricide is problematic will inevitably be a factor in interpreting *Electra*. Sophocles was not of course committed to presenting the issue in the same way that Aeschylus had done, but he would have needed to take positive steps to distance himself from his predecessor's version. This would require at least some recognition of the fact that the matricide was potentially a problem, even if he then proceeded to justify it (as outlined by Winnington-Ingram in the previous paragraph). It was also pointed out in Chapter 2 that the mad Orestes pursued by the Furies appears several times in Euripides, and that by the time of Sophocles' *Electra* he had become a byword for a violent madman. This evidence for the tradition tends to be overlooked by advocates of the affirmative interpretation who focus too exclusively on Aeschylus.

Jebb pointed to Homer's *Odyssey* for an entirely positive view of Orestes' revenge. Some questions were raised about this in Chapter 2. There is also a crucial difference of genre between the *Odyssey* and *Electra*. It is a notable feature of Homer's style that he had little interest in violence within the family, and tended to gloss over it when he touched on stories where it traditionally featured. Fifth-century tragedy, on the other hand, typically focusses on violence within the family (often involving women), and on the political effects of such violence. This is invariably problematic, even in those cases where it is eventually resolved. Most of the surviving tragedies come into this category, and it is striking that the tragedians sometimes go out of their way to introduce a familial aspect into stories where it had not previously been prominent. An example is the story of the burial of the bodies of the warriors who tried to restore Polynices to the throne of Thebes ('the seven against Thebes'). Athenian patriotic myth stressed the role of Athens in ensuring that the bodies were buried. Sophocles' treatment in *Antigone*, on the other hand, attributes this initiative to a female member of the Theban royal family acting in defiance of male authority in both her family and her city. This type of story, relating domestic strife to political disorder, is typical of fifth-century tragedy, and is of course present in *Electra*. Violence within the family is the stuff of tragedy, and all the evidence suggests that it is simply not possible in the genre for the problems associated with such violence not to be central to the plays. There is certainly no parallel for it being unproblematic. Medea (in Euripides' *Medea*) may escape retaliation for her revenge on Jason and his new family, but the murder of her sons is only committed after prolonged indecision (*Medea* 1021-80), and at terrible and permanent cost to herself (*Medea* 1242-50). *Electra* would be unique among surviving tragedies if it presented an act of violence within the family – and especially one as serious as matricide – as intrinsically unproblematic.

Other scholars argue that the play is full of hints that the killing of Clytemnestra and Aegisthus cannot be final. A sophisticated version of this approach was developed by Winnington-Ingram. He argued that Sophocles treats retaliatory justice ('Fury-justice') in a fundamentally Aeschylean way, with the implication that every avenger is liable to retaliation in turn. This complex of ideas is evoked by the very mention of the Furies. They are mentioned by name on four occasions in the play (112, 276, 491, 1080), and alluded to once (1388). It thus cannot be said that Sophocles has 'omitted the Furies'. The first *stasimon* (472-515) associates the Furies with the succession of sorrows which has afflicted the house of Pelops since his murder of Myrtilus, and which there is no reason to suppose will stop now (10, 515, 1498). Electra appeals to the law of retaliation, and it will inevitably apply also to her (245-50,

577-83). There is a series of references towards the end of the play to 'completion' (1344, 1397, 1399, 1417, 1435, 1464), including its very last word (1510), but this only raises the question of whether this really is the end. Winnington-Ingram does not rely on any future appearance of the Furies: 'It is not the future fate of Orestes (and Electra) which matters; it is not what the Furies may do when the play is over that matters, but what they have done and do before and during the play' (p. 227). Electra herself is 'the victim and the agent of the Furies' (p. 235).

T.C.W. Stinton objected to Winnington-Ingram that mention of the Furies may signify revenge, but does not necessarily evoke an Aeschylean cycle of retaliation (pp. 465-79). Electra and Orestes rely on justice and the command of Apollo (32-7, 70, 1264-70), rather than on the *lex talionis* (the principle of an eye for an eye). The Furies pursue unjust killers, but just retribution can indeed be final. Stinton argues that Myrtilus is mentioned as the beginning of evils, but with no mention of his curse or implication of Aeschylean ideas of inherited sin. He may be right that these ideas are not specifically Aeschylean, but there remains the sense of continuous suffering afflicting the house, of which the present events are just one more instalment. It does not answer the question to say that Orestes and Electra rely on justice rather than simply on the *lex talionis*. Clytemnestra also appeals to justice. The question remains of whether her guilt requires her to be killed – and by her children. Castor in Euripides' *Electra* agrees that she deserved to die, but insists that Orestes was wrong to kill her (1244; cf. *Orestes* 538-9).

Apollo

There are two key passages near the end of the play which have been thought to cast doubt on the success of the matricide. The first of them is when the bloodied Orestes comes out of the palace, and Electra asks him 'Orestes, how have these things turned out?' He replies: 'Things within the house are well, if Apollo prophesied well' (1424-5). This reply has been much discussed because it is the only possible hint in the play of the doubts which Orestes came to feel about the deed in Aeschylus and Euripides (Aeschylus, *Libation Bearers* 1016-17; Euripides *Electra* 1190-3). The question is how much doubt is implied by the conditional. Scholars have cited convincing parallels for these conditional clauses having the sense 'if (as I am confident) ...'. One such is the prediction of the aged Oedipus that his corpse will drink the blood of his enemies 'if Zeus is still Zeus, and Apollo the son of Zeus speaks truly' (Sophocles, *Oedipus at Colonus* 623). Oedipus is expressing confidence, not doubt. On the other hand, these conditionals express awareness of the inscrutability of the gods and the unreliability of their human interpreters (cf. *Ajax* 746, 783). No mortal can interpret the gods' utterances or predict their actions with complete certainty. Orestes may be confident, but his formulation acknowledges the element of doubt which attends all statements about the gods.[2]

It is another matter whether Orestes' statement has a wider significance which is invisible to him. Apollo's oracle is denounced as 'unwise' at Euripides' *Electra* 1246, and the god is criticized elsewhere in Euripides (e.g. *Andromache* 1161-5). In Aeschylus' *Oresteia*, his oracle is shown to be only partially correct, and he appears in a somewhat unflattering light in *Eumenides*. The question 'if Apollo prophesied well' is too prominent in the story for all elements of doubt to be expelled from Orestes' statement here. The mere fact that he ordered the matricide cannot be the last word on its justice. Mary Whitlock Blundell writes: 'we cannot assume that the playwright's approval is coextensive with that of Apollo. The interests of different divinities may themselves conflict. It was Artemis, Apollo's twin sister, who initiated the whole cycle of killings, in return for an apparently trivial offence' (pp. 182-3). It is remarkable that any further consideration of the matter is cut short by the appearance of Aegisthus (1428). This leaves no room for the madness and despair which afflict Orestes at exactly this point in Aeschylus' and Euripides' versions of the story.

6. Matricide

'The present and the future woes of the Pelopidae'

The second key passage which has been thought to cast doubt on the success of the matricide is the exchange that takes place shortly before Orestes takes Aegisthus into the palace to kill him (1495-1500):

> ORESTES: Go where you killed my father, so that you may die in the same place.
> AEGISTHUS: Is it really necessary for this house to witness the present and the future woes of the Pelopidae?
> ORESTES: It will witness yours, at least; of that much I am an expert prophet.
> AEGISTHUS: Your father lacked the skill of which you boast.

Aegisthus' reference to 'the future woes of the Pelopidae' (1498) is the jewel in the crown of the ironic interpretation, since it seems to refer to the imminent pursuit of Orestes by the Furies. The revenge would thus be neither as justified nor as successful as it may have seemed, and Orestes' apparent triumph will soon turn to torment. The passage has in consequence been the target of attempts by advocates of the affirmative interpretation to play down its significance. Some of them argue that the reference is only to Aegisthus' own imminent death. This is refuted both by the general terms of his statement and by the limitative 'at least' in Orestes' reply, which indicates that he understands him to be making a broader claim.[3] Other scholars argue that Aegisthus refers only to woes witnessed by the palace, which is not where the pursuit of Orestes by the Furies traditionally took place (e.g. Szlezák, p. 18). This seems a shade pedantic, since the expression is figurative and the point is the continuity of the sufferings of the family, rather than what the actual building may literally be supposed to 'see'. Finally, it is argued that Aegisthus has no way of knowing what will happen to Orestes in the future. P.T. Stevens thus thinks that his words are 'no more than a vague threat in the hope of disconcerting Orestes' (p. 113).

Aegisthus is certainly threatening Orestes, as we shall see, but his words also have an application to himself. One of Sophocles' favourite themes is a character's discovery, at the climax of his suffering, of the true pattern of his life. Oedipus' final insight is marked by the outburst 'It has all come true!' (*Oedipus the King* 1182), while Heracles' understanding of his fate is completed by the mention of Nessus: 'Now I understand in what a calamity I stand' (*Women of Trachis* 1145). Aegisthus falls far short of the tragic stature of an Oedipus or a Heracles, but he nevertheless experiences some sort of tragic *anagnôrisis*, or recognition. He is a Pelopid, and he glimpses here that the murder of Agamemnon was not the final act in the unhappy history of the family (cf. 504-15). His own death is part of a larger pattern.

J.T. Sheppard remarked, 'Dying men, they say, speak truth'.[4] He did not elaborate, and the point has often been overlooked. A good parallel can be found in Socrates' final speech at his trial (399 BC): 'I want now to prophesy to those of you who voted against me; for I am at the point of death, when prophecy comes most readily. I tell you, you men who have killed me, that immediately after my death you will suffer punishment far harsher than your execution of me' (Plato, *Apology* 39c). A dying man has particular authority in predicting suffering for his killer. Patroclus addresses his last words to Hector: 'You yourself will not live long, but already death and strong fate are standing beside you, to bring you down at the hands of Achilles' (Homer, *Iliad* 16.852-4). Patroclus is right, as is Hector himself when his dying words predict that Achilles will be killed 'by Paris and Apollo, at the Scaean gates' (Homer, *Iliad* 22.359-60). Homer does not feel the need to explain how Patroclus and Hector have obtained this information. Euripides prefers to rationalize such knowledge, as dying or maimed characters suddenly recall oracles predicting suffering for their enemies (*Cyclops* 696-700, *Children of Heracles* 1026-44, *Hecuba* 1259-

86). The addressee typically dismisses such predictions with a taunt, as does Orestes in *Electra*.

Deborah Roberts has discussed how all seven of Sophocles' surviving plays contain an allusive reference to the future beyond the events of the play.[5] An example is Hyllus' remark at the end of *Women of Trachis* that 'no one foresees what is to come' (1270). He is in the process of taking his father Heracles to his funeral pyre on Mt Oeta, and there has been much debate about whether we should see an allusion to the well-known myth of Heracles' apotheosis. How far should this be allowed to qualify the pessimistic tone of the end of the play, and in particular Hyllus' bitter criticisms of Zeus? Compare the hints at the end of *Oedipus at Colonus* that Antigone will be required to bury the body of her brother Polynices (1407-10, 1769-72). We know from *Antigone* that she will die as a result. Oedipus' curse on his hated sons will thus lead indirectly to the death of his beloved daughter. How far does this qualify our response to his behaviour in the play and to the apparently peaceful and harmonious nature of his death? Roberts herself stresses both the element of finality in these endings (Heracles and Oedipus go off to their deaths, Electra is freed from oppression), and the 'anti-closural' way in which allusions to future events disrupt that finality. The story itself may be complete, but the nature of human life means that it is inevitably part of a larger story.

Roberts offers a subtle, and in many ways convincing, account of these allusions to future events in Sophocles. The problems, however, may be somewhat more acute than she recognizes. Some of the allusions which she discusses are not merely to 'another story', but are highly relevant to prominent themes in the plays themselves. This distinguishes Sophocles' endings from the ending of Homer's *Iliad*, which she cites, where there is a reference to the war continuing after the burial of Hector (24.666-7). This can plausibly be regarded as 'another story', which does not substantially qualify our understanding of the *Iliad* itself. In *Women of Trachis*, however, the apotheosis of Heracles would imply a completely different view of Zeus to that being voiced at the end of the play. If Antigone's departure to Thebes at the end of *Oedipus at Colonus* is taken to imply her death as a result of burying Polynices, our understanding of Oedipus' treatment of his children would inevitably be affected, especially as it is criticized both by Theseus (592) and by Antigone herself (1181-1203). The possibility of a conclusive act of violence is one of the main themes of *Electra*. Orestes, Electra, and the chorus all believe that the killing of Clytemnestra and Aegisthus is indeed final. Any future pursuit of Orestes by the Furies would not merely be another story, but a demonstration that the revenge is not in fact conclusive.

Irony in Sophocles

An ironic interpretation of *Electra* may seem to gain support from Sophocles' use of irony other plays. The concept of dramatic irony (i.e. exploitation of the contrast between what seems to be the case and what really is the case) did indeed originate in the interpretation of Sophocles.[6] It has been objected that there is a significant difference between the kind of irony which is proposed by the ironic interpretation of *Electra* and that which is generally associated with Sophocles. P.T. Stevens writes, 'elsewhere in Sophocles at any rate such irony is an incidental contribution to the total effect and never contradicts the natural impression of the play as a whole' (p. 112). There are two features which distinguish the more usual type of Sophoclean irony. In the first place, the audience knows from the start the truth which is hidden from the characters in the play. In *Oedipus the King*, for example, the audience is aware that Oedipus himself is the unknown murderer for whom he is searching, that he curses himself, and that Tiresias' accusations are correct. The tragic irony would be ineffective if the audience did not know the true state of affairs. Secondly, the tragic character must at some point discover the truth. This will be a climactic moment in the play, as indeed is Oedipus' *anagnôrisis* mentioned in the previous section (*Oedipus the King* 1182). Such irony occurs in *Electra* as a result of Electra's ignorance that Orestes has returned, but she is in the end

110

reunited with him. The final scene is suffused with irony at the expense of Aegisthus, but he eventually discovers the truth which the audience has known all along (1479-80). Evidently the type of irony proposed by supporters of the ironic interpretation of *Electra* is not of this type. The audience has no definite knowledge that events have a meaning which has been concealed from Orestes and Electra, and there is no moment of revelation when they come to realize what it is.

Tragic irony, as discussed in the previous paragraph, is not the only kind of irony in Sophocles. It would be a poor reader or spectator of his plays who expected everything to be spelled out explicitly. This can be illustrated briefly from his treatment of Apollo in *Oedipus the King*. Tiresias says to Oedipus: 'You are not fated to fall at my hand, since Apollo will take care of this, and he is sufficient' (376-7). Oedipus himself, after he has blinded himself, blames Apollo: 'This was Apollo, my friends, Apollo, who accomplished these cruel, cruel sufferings of mine' (1329-30). But what has Apollo actually done? John Gould writes: 'Apollo's presence in the play presents a paradox. His participation in Oedipus' experience is undeniable; it would pass all limits of a reasonable suspension of belief to doubt that .... And yet ... Apollo is not seen to act on the human stage of the play at all, and it requires us to press the text of Sophocles' drama beyond conviction to be sure we have detected his hand in the precise guidance of what occurs' (p. 261). Sophocles creates an intensely strong sense of Apollo's involvement, while leaving it largely obscure what he has actually done. It is still less clear what his motives are, or whether there is any larger pattern into which his activities fit. The irony implicates the audience as much as the characters, and is not resolved in any unambiguous revelation of the truth.

Antigone offers some illuminating parallels to Sophocles' handling of the tragic issues in *Electra*. The German philosopher G.W.F. Hegel (1770-1831) famously analysed *Antigone* as a clash of two equal, but partial, sets of values. Antigone represents family love and the law of the nether gods, while Creon defends the law of the state:

Creon is not a tyrant, but really a moral power; Creon is not in the wrong; he maintains that the law of the State, the authority of government, is to be held in respect, and that punishment follows the infraction of the law. Each of these two sides realizes only one of the moral powers, and has only one of these as its content; this is the element of one-sidedness here, and the meaning of eternal justice is shown in this, that both end in injustice just because they are one-sided, though at the same time both obtain justice too. Both are recognized as having a value of their own in the untroubled course of morality.[7]

The problem with this interpretation is that Creon does indeed turn out to be a tyrant, whose right to speak for the *polis* (city-state) is questionable (e.g. 690-700, 733-9). He eventually admits that his prohibition of the burial of Polynices was a disastrous mistake, and ends the play a broken man. Hegel's description of him is thus manifestly incorrect. Brian Vickers summarizes his lively critique of Hegel's view as follows: 'It is not a collision between two "equally justified" aspects of the ethical substance, for although Antigone fulfils Hegel's criterion of representing truly ethical powers Creon is never allowed to meet the conflict on anything other than his own authoritarian sadistic plane.'[8]

Hegel's interpretation cannot, however, be dismissed quite so easily. Creon begins by emphasizing the primacy of the *polis* over private relationships (175-91), and his sentiments were endorsed in the fourth century by Demosthenes (19.247). Thucydides put similar views in the mouth of Pericles in a speech delivered in 430 BC: 'I believe that individuals profit more from the prosperity of the whole city than by gaining personal benefit in a context of public misfortune. Private prosperity will be brought down along with a disaster befalling the state, while there is a much better chance of finding some remedy for private misfortune if the state is prosperous' (2.60; cf. Pericles' funeral speech, 2.35-46; also Socrates at Plato, *Crito* 51a). There can be no doubt that such ideas were widely accepted in late fifth-century Athens, and that they could have given Sophocles the materials to create a much stronger Creon than he actually has done. Creon is not only wrong, but far worse than he needed to be. This makes it more difficult to assess Antigone that it would have been if her opponent's position had been more soundly based. Creon may indeed deserve to be opposed, but how are we to react to Antigone's complete failure to consider at any stage that the *polis* might reasonably command some loyalty? Sophocles' refusal to allow this issue to be articulated is reinforced by the lack of any discussion (e.g. by Tiresias) of what she has done after her final departure from the stage. There may thus be a Hegelian conflict after all, although Creon fails to give adequate expression to the *polis* side of it. The values of the *polis* are a significant absence, distorted by Creon and ignored by Antigone.

The Orestes myth contained abundant material for Hegelian treatment. Aeschylus presented the myth in exactly this fashion in the *Oresteia*, as Hegel himself was quick to note.[9] The matricide involves a whole series of conflicts: man *v.* woman, new gods *v.* old gods, marriage *v.* parenthood, social ties *v.* natural relationships. These conflicts are eventually resolved by a trial in *Eumenides* under the supervision of Athena. In *Electra*, as in *Antigone*, Sophocles avoids treating the issues in any such way. Clytemnestra is made as bad as possible, and she carries none of the weight of significance which she has in the *Oresteia*. Orestes and Electra, on the other hand, fail as completely to consider the problems of matricide as Antigone does the claims of the *polis* in *Antigone*. Sophocles gives the fullest weight to one side of the equation, that Clytemnestra deserves to die, but gives no explicit expression to the other side, that Orestes cannot kill her. He does what he often does elsewhere, which is to leave inexplicit what is in fact the main point of the play. It should be stressed that the interpretation being sketched here is not 'ironic' in the sense that it denies any of the overt meaning of the play. Clytemnestra and Aegisthus are indeed very bad, and deserve to be killed. The point, rather, is that there is more to the play than its overt meaning.

The end

The play ends with Orestes taking Aegisthus into the palace to kill him. Supporters of the affirmative interpretation argue that the death of this obvious villain is a positive note on which to conclude, and that there is no reason to think that there are any further sufferings in store for Orestes and Electra. On the other hand, Sophocles could have done a lot more to emphasize that the ending is indeed triumphant. Oliver Taplin writes: 'Sophokles could, after all, have ended the play with both Klytaimnestra and Aigisthos safely dead, finally sending Orestes off as the reinstated king with a chorus-supported victory procession.'[10]

Sophocles ends the play on a note of incompletion and suspense. He does this by exploiting two tragic conventions in particular. First, it is common in tragedy for someone to be verbally defeated or mocked on stage before being taken inside to be killed. This happens in Aeschylus' *Agamemnon* and *Libation Bearers*, and in Euripides' *Electra* and *Heracles*. There are variations on the pattern in Euripides' *Cyclops*, *Medea*, *Hecuba*, and *Orestes*. The victims' cries are typically heard from inside the *skênê* soon after they have gone in, to be followed by a display of their corpses. It is thus remarkable that Sophocles' *Electra* ends immediately after Orestes has taken Aegisthus inside. There is no doubt that Aegisthus will be killed, but the audience is left waiting for his death cries.

Secondly, there is not the remotest parallel in extant tragedy for a play ending with something significant about to happen inside the *skênê*. It is common enough, as was noted above, for significant events somewhere else to be imminent at the end. Euripides' *Children of Heracles*, indeed, ends with the villain Eurystheus being taken off to be killed. Inside the *skênê*, however, funerals may be arranged and life may continue (as in *Antigone*), but there will certainly not be any violence in the immediate future. It is relatively rare for there even to be an exit into the *skênê* at the end of a tragedy, and much more common for everyone to depart by an *eisodos* and the place to be vacated altogether. A rule-proving exception is the defiance

114

of Clytemnestra and Aegisthus as they go into the palace at the end of Aeschylus' *Agamemnon*, which is the first play of a connected trilogy and leaves a strong sense that there is more to come. The reason for this convention is that in the Greek theatre the dramatist needed to mark the end of a play without the benefit of the curtain and house-lights of the modern theatre. The actors depart, and the audience is left looking at the *skênê*. It is highly unsettling for significant events to be due to take place there when the play has finished. Orestes takes Aegisthus into the palace, presumably followed by Electra, the chorus chooses to march off at this apparently interesting moment, and the play ends.

Sophocles thus makes skilful use of the conventions of the Greek tragic stage to end *Electra* with a powerful sense of incompletion, which undercuts the chorus's final word 'completed'. This is the second interruption in his presentation of the murders, since the initial appearance of Aegisthus cut short further reaction to the killing of Clytemnestra. The significance of this lack of closure should not be narrowed down to the question of whether the Furies are about to appear. Aeschylus followed Orestes' fate through pursuit by the Furies to trial in Athens and eventual acquittal. A similar future is predicted by Castor at the end of Euripides' *Electra*, although it brings no consolation to Orestes and Electra. Sophocles leaves us with nothing so specific, but rather with a curtailed reaction to the murder of Clytemnestra, the uncompleted murder of Aegisthus, and the prospect of 'the future woes of the Pelopidae'.

Afterlife

Electra has been one of the most frequently performed of all Greek tragedies. This chapter is an attempt to give some impression of what it has meant to audiences and performers at various times and places. It begins with a survey of the tantalizing anecdotes about the play which survive from antiquity. Much more could have been said about its performance history since the Renaissance, and it has been necessary to focus on a representative selection of modern productions. The Electra myth generally has had immense influence on the modern stage, and three major works have been based on Sophocles' version in particular. Voltaire's *Oreste* (1750) is an attempt to adapt it to the conventions of French classical tragedy. Hofmannsthal's *Elektra* (1903), by contrast, is a study in extreme psychology which can be related to the early works of Freud. It provided the libretto for the best-known opera based on a Greek tragedy, Richard Strauss' *Elektra* (1909). The Hofmannsthal-Strauss Electra may have overshadowed her Sophoclean original in the twentieth century, but there have also been times when the play's politics have seemed as interesting as its psychology. Problems of style have been recurrent, and *Electra* as much as any play has been a test-case of the viability of Greek tragedy on the modern stage.

Electra in antiquity

Sophocles was the most successful of the tragedians in his lifetime, and remained popular in the century after his death. The festival of Dionysus in Athens included revivals of old tragedies from 386 BC, and there were also many lesser festivals

at which Sophocles' plays would have been performed. Demosthenes' speech *On the False Embassy* (343 BC) refers to
frequent performances of *Antigone* featuring the star actors
Theodorus and Aristodemus, in which his adversary Aeschines
took lesser roles (19.246-7). There was an international circuit,
and the leading actors commanded high fees. They would no
doubt have been drawn to plays, like *Electra*, which offered
them attractive roles. Anecdotes about their performances cir-
culated long after their deaths. One of the most famous, told by
Aulus Gellius (*c.* AD 180), concerns a performance of *Electra*.
The actor Polus had returned to the Athenian stage after a
period of mourning for the death of a son. 'Polus, dressed in the
mourning clothes of Electra, took from its tomb the urn containing the ashes of his son. He embraced it as if it held the ashes
of Orestes, and filled the theatre not with the semblance of
sorrow, but with genuine and unfeigned lamentation. Thus,
while it appeared that a play was being performed, it was in fact
real grief which was enacted' (*Attic Nights* 6.5). This story,
recounted some 500 years after the event, testifies both to the
fame of the scene and to the uncanny emotional authenticity of
a great actor.[1]

Cephisodorus, a pupil of the orator Isocrates (436-338 BC),
included *Electra* 61 ('no word is bad if it is profitable') among
the ignoble sentiments to be found in the works of the great
poets (Athenaeus 122c). Drama has always been a rich source
of memorable sayings which can be abstracted from their original context, and ancient writers regularly attribute opinions to
the dramatists themselves which are expressed by characters
in their plays ('Sophocles says ...'). Aristotle (384-22 BC) offers
somewhat more sophisticated criticism of *Electra* when he remarks on the illogicality of the reference to the Pythian games
in the Paedagogus' messenger speech (*Poetics* 1460a31-2). The
point seems to be that the games were not instituted until 582
BC, long after the period in which the play is set. Aristotle
compliments Sophocles for confining this anachronism to reported speech. It would evidently have been worse if it had
involved stage action.

Electra continued to be well-known in the third century, and would no doubt have been performed all over the Greek world by the powerful guilds of itinerant Greek actors known as the Artists of Dionysus. Machon, a comic poet active in Alexandria in the middle of the century, wrote a book of verse containing anecdotes about famous Athenian courtesans. One of them concerns a response by the famously witty Mania to Demetrius Poliorcetes (336-283 BC), king of Macedonia. She demanded a gift before granting a particular sexual favour. She received the gift, and then quoted the second line of *Electra*, 'son of Agamemnon, now it is possible for you ...' (Athenaeus 579a). A similar story is told about the wife of the fourth-century actor Theodorus, who refused to sleep with him while he was preparing for a dramatic contest, but welcomed him home with this line when he eventually returned victorious (Plutarch, *Moralia* 737b). It is not stated whether his victory was in *Electra*. Somewhat more edifying is an epigram by Dioscorides (late third century), which imagines a conversation between a passer-by and the statue of an actor on the tomb of Sophocles. The actor is holding the mask known as 'the girl with shaven hair', conventionally used to play characters in mourning. The passer-by asks which play she is from. The actor replies: 'If you want to call her Antigone you would not go wrong, or Electra too; for both are supreme' (*Palatine Anthology* 7.37). Sophocles' definitive creation is the mourning girl, whichever of the two plays she belongs to.

Electra was not only widely performed in this period, but also benefited from the academic work in Alexandria which is the foundation of our texts of the play. The first scholarly edition of Sophocles is generally ascribed to Aristophanes of Byzantium (*c.* 257-180 BC), librarian at Alexandria from *c.* 195 BC. He would have used, among other manuscripts, the official Athenian text established by Lycurgus (*c.* 330 BC). Aristophanes would have known most of Sophocles' 120 or more plays, but by the third century AD it seems that only seven of his plays (including *Electra*) were generally known. The use of these seven plays as set books in schools will have played a considerable part in ensuring their survival.

The Romans first encountered serious drama when they conquered the Greek cities of South Italy and Sicily in the middle of the third century BC. Sophocles was one of the classic playwrights whose works were produced in this region by the Artists of Dionysus. The first plays in Latin were staged in 240 BC by Livius Andronicus, a Greek from Tarentum. Roman dramatists based their plays on Greek models, but greatly reduced the role of the chorus. *Electra* was translated into Latin by Atilius, apparently in the early second century BC. Cicero mentions this work in 45 BC in the course of an attack on those who despise even the more distinguished Latin versions of Greek originals: 'I disagree with them so strongly that, although Sophocles' *Electra* is a masterpiece, I still think that Atilius' bad translation of it is worth reading' (*De Finibus* 1.2). Cicero seems to have regarded Atilius' style as wooden. An excerpt from his *Electra* was one of two tragic passages sung at the funeral of Julius Caesar in 44 BC, with a view to arousing pity and indignation for his murder (Suetonius, *Julius* 84). Suetonius does not identify the passage, but Electra's opening lament for Agamemnon would have provided suitable material (cf. Sophocles, *Electra* 86-120). It is fascinating that Greek tragedy, albeit mediated through a Latin translation, was thought to give appropriate formulation to the powerful emotions which were felt at this intensely significant moment in Roman history. *Electra* supplies the paradigmatic expression of grief for a leader treacherously murdered. There are precedents as far back as the fourth century for this kind of exploitation of parallels between tragedy and public life, which was no doubt made easier by actors performing set-pieces extracted from their original contexts.

A few years later, we find *Electra* providing the paradigm for private rather than public emotion (*c.* 26 BC). Propertius, trying to find words for his satisfaction after a good night with his mistress, lists four examples from Greek mythology of supreme joy following upon prolonged anxiety and frustration. One of these is Electra, 'when she saw Orestes safe, for whom she had wept when she thought that she held his bones' (2.14.5-6). Propertius alludes to mythical figures rather than to specific literary works, but his image of Electra derives originally from Sophocles' creation.

Voltaire's *Oreste* (1750)

Sophocles' *Electra* was preferred to Aeschylus' and Euripides' versions of the story in eighteenth-century France, and had been translated (1693) by André Dacier as an illustration of the principles of Aristotle. Dacier thought that deliberate matricide was 'atrocious', and would have to be toned down if the story were to be suitable for the French stage. Pierre Brumoy, who included a translation of *Electra* in his influential guide to Greek tragedy (1730), also argued that the matricide was revolting. He thought that this was only partly mitigated in Sophocles by his insistence that Clytemnestra is exceptionally bad and that the matricide is commanded by the gods.

Voltaire's version of Sophocles' *Electra* had two notable predecessors. The first was by Hilaire-Bernard Roquelyne, Baron de Longpierre (1659-1721). His *Electre* (1702) focussed the revenge plot on Aegisthus, and followed the advice of Dacier in having Orestes kill Clytemnestra by mistake in the act of killing Aegisthus.[2] He nevertheless loses his reason as a result. The play was well received at its initial private performances in Versailles, but failed when it was performed in public in Paris many years later (1719). Prosper Jolyot de Crébillon (1674-1762) catered more to contemporary tastes by including some love-interest in his *Electre* (1708), supplying Aegisthus with a son and a daughter from a previous marriage with whom Electra and Orestes respectively are in love. He introduced various other complications, but followed Longpierre in making the killing of Clytemnestra accidental. She curses Orestes, and he goes mad. The famous actress Adrienne Lecouvreur (1692-1730) made her debut at the Comédie-Française some years later in the title role (1717). Crébillon's *Electre* was a great success, but Voltaire despised it and was determined to show that he could treat the same subject in a less meretricious fashion.

Voltaire (1694-1778) wanted to 'turn the French into Athenians' by putting on tragedies without the love-interest ('galanterie') and excessive complexity which had hitherto been regarded as indispensable in French tragedy, and focussing on the proper tragic emotions of pity and fear. Crébillon's melodramatic plays, Voltaire thought, aroused 'horreur' rather than 'terreur'. His *Oreste* (1750) followed the versions of Longpierre and Crébillon in having Orestes kill Clytemnestra by mistake, but in all three dramatists this has the unfortunate effect of eliminating the main tragic point of the story.[3] Voltaire tried to make up for this by representing the accident as a punishment for Orestes' disobedience of a divine command not to reveal himself to Electra until after he has killed Aegisthus. This is not a very satisfactory solution, not least because the punishment seems so disproportionate to the offence. Voltaire gives Aegisthus a son, called Plistène (i.e. Pleisthenes, a name which features in Aegisthus' family in Greek myth), who never actually appears but plays a part in diversifying the action. Aegisthus hopes to unify the family by marrying him off to Electra, but he has in fact been killed by Orestes before the play begins. Voltaire otherwise offers a free adaptation of Sophocles' characters and dramatic situations to the requirements of the French stage. Electra's grief and heroism are recognizable from Sophocles, as are the contrast with a weaker sister (here called Iphise). There are also precedents in Sophocles for the festival celebrating Agamemnon's death, the urn supposedly containing Orestes' ashes (but which here contains those of Plistène), and the protracted irony surrounding Electra's ignorance of Orestes' survival and return.

Voltaire's most notable contribution is his development of the character of Clytemnestra. She is loyal to Aegisthus, but now bitterly regrets her crimes: 'Marriage, fatal marriage, crime which prospered for so long, / The bloody knots which murder and adultery have tied' (I.iv.269-70). She may be provoked by Electra's outbursts of hostility, but cannot entirely suppress her love for her children. She tries to save Orestes from Aegisthus, but is then killed trying to save Aegisthus from Orestes. Voltaire was aware that Euripides had already presented a gentler Clytemnestra than Sophocles', and he takes this considerably further. He also seems to have been influenced by Euripides in his expansion of the role of Pylades. Pylades does not speak in Sophocles' or Euripides' *Electras*, but Voltaire's portrayal of his devotion to Orestes owes much to Euripides' *Iphigenia among the Taurians* and *Orestes*. Voltaire's paedagogus figure, called Pammène, resembles his counterpart in Euripides rather than in Sophocles, in that he does not accompany Orestes into exile, but rather lives in exile within the territory of Argos (cf. Euripides, *Electra* 409-12). Voltaire's account of the popular uprising which overthrows Aegisthus may owe something to the enthusiastic reception that his retainers gave Orestes at Euripides, *Electra* 847-55. The play ends, as in Euripides, with Orestes being driven into exile by the Furies.

Voltaire's sympathetic portrait of Clytemnestra means that the weight of villainy rests firmly on the shoulders of Aegisthus, who is represented as a powerful and unscrupulous tyrant. On the other hand, he is in no way ridiculous or contemptible, and even evokes some sympathy on account of the death of his son Plistène. The play as a whole, like French classical tragedy generally, obeys Aristotle's injunction that the characters of tragedy should be basically good. It has a relentless high-mindedness, with god-fearing characters mostly trying hard to do the right thing. This is no doubt why the loyal and upstanding Pylades was such a popular figure in French tragedy. Racine's *Andromaque* (1667) also gives him a role which he did not have in the Euripidean model. Electra may hate Clytemnestra, but is still capable of seeing some good in her. The contrast with Hofmannsthal's *Elektra* could not be more extreme.

Hofmannsthal's *Elektra* (1903)

Hugo von Hofmannsthal's *Elektra*, 'freely adapted after Sophocles', was first performed in Berlin on 30 October 1903. The director was Max Reinhardt (1873-1943), and the part of Electra was taken by Gertrud Eysoldt (1870-1955).[4] Hofmannsthal (1874-1929) was already well-known as a lyric poet. He had, however, come to feel that words alone could not express what he wanted to say, and that as a writer and as an individual he was cut off from society at large. His response to this crisis was to write for the stage, and in particular to exploit the resonance and universality of Greek myth. *Elektra* was the first product of this new approach, and was followed by other plays on classical subjects. Greek tragedy had indeed been regarded since the Renaissance as the ideal of the complete work of art, combining poetry, music, and dance, and enjoying an enviable cultural centrality in the society from which it sprang.[5]

The structure and proportions of *Elektra* are based quite closely on Sophocles, although there are a few omissions and additions. Hofmannsthal omits the non-speaking role of Pylades, and delays the appearance of Orestes until the recognition scene. The Paedagogus' messenger speech is also omitted, and his part is reduced to a mere five lines. One result of all this is to make *Elektra* an even more intensely female work, with almost no male voices before Orestes' first words at line 884. Hofmannsthal also omits Sophocles' chorus, depriving Electra of any social interaction with sympathetic outsiders.

Hofmannsthal adds two scenes involving servants. The opening dialogue between the serving-maids prepares for the appearance of the alarming heroine in a rather similar way to the first act of Euripides' *Medea*. The scene with the servants and the cook is a comic interlude at an intensely serious point of the play, of a kind which is familiar in Shakespeare but which also has precedents in Greek tragedy (e.g. Cilissa in Aeschylus' *Libation Bearers*). Most of these servants are hostile to Electra, which emphasizes her solitude and degradation. Sophocles' Clytemnestra defends what she has done, while Hofmannsthal's is a study in repression and neurosis. Her decadence may seem distinctively *fin de siècle*, but she also owes something to the luxury of Euripides' Clytemnestra (Euripides, *Electra* 966, 1071). Electra's exaggerated deference also has precedent in Euripides (*Electra* 1004-10, 1139-40), in particular her comparison of Clytemnestra to the gods (*Electra* 994-5).[6] Hofmannsthal continues the play to the death of Aegisthus, after which there is an account of the triumph of Orestes. The most significant difference of all is that Electra celebrates with a maenadic dance, after which she collapses lifeless. Hofmannsthal indicates 'silence' before the final curtain, with no response to Chrysothemis' desperate cries for Orestes. He thus concludes on an ambiguous and somewhat troubling note. A projected sequel, *Orestes in Delphi*, was never written.

Hofmannsthal was anxious to distance his play from the humane and idealistic Hellenism epitomized by Goethe's *Iphigenie auf Tauris* (1787). He insisted that its setting and costumes should avoid antiquarian evocation of ancient Greece ('antikisieren'). German classical scholarship in the later nineteenth century had already done much to undermine old-fashioned views that the Greeks, and especially Sophocles, were imperturbably serene and balanced.[7] Contemporary and later criticisms of Hofmannsthal's perversion of his Greek model are often based on a sentimental view of Sophocles and of Greek culture generally which was outdated even in 1903. Hofmannsthal almost entirely suppresses any indication that the action takes place in Greece, and the location is simply 'the palace'. There is no mention of the earlier history of the family, or of the other myths which are prominent in Sophocles (e.g. Niobe). The sacrifice of Iphigenia is passed over, depriving Clytemnestra of any justification for killing Agamemnon. Orestes' task has been imposed upon him by 'the gods', but there is no mention of Apollo or of any other individual god. Hofmannsthal evokes a pre-classical or even oriental world, which has distinct similarities to the court of Herod in Oscar Wilde's *Salome*.

Hofmannsthal's play is set in the inner courtyard, at the back of the palace. Servants' quarters and a well are visible. The setting is domestic and enclosed, in contrast to the setting of Sophocles' play at the front of the palace where it meets the outside world. Hofmannsthal follows Greek precedent in avoiding scene changes, keeping the murders off stage, and focussing attention on the door into the palace. Characters come and go from outside the palace through the courtyard gate on the left. Hofmannsthal departs from Greek staging practice in using windows through which events inside the palace are sometimes visible. He turned to drama to exploit non-verbal means of expression, and his stage-directions prescribe lighting-effects and costume, as well as a range of significant actions and gestures. The stage-direction for Orestes' appearance reads as follows: 'Orestes stands in the courtyard door, his figure set off in black against the last gleam of light. He enters. Electra looks at him. He turns slowly around so that his glance falls on her. Electra starts up violently; she trembles.' Hofmannsthal's determination to move beyond the merely verbal is nowhere clearer than at the end of the play, where the weight of meaning is carried by Electra's dance.

Hofmannsthal's treatment of the characters evidently makes use of the insights of psychoanalysis.[8] He knew some of the early work of Freud, although it would be a mistake to relate his characters too closely to individual case studies. His blending of psychoanalysis and myth is clearest in his portrayal of Clytemnestra, who has repressed her guilt and suffers from terrifying dreams. She has no memory of the murder: 'Now it was / before, and then it was past – in between / I did nothing'. She seeks advice from Electra as from a psychoanalyst. Electra terrorizes her much more blatantly than she does in Sophocles, and Clytemnestra only allows this because she is desperate for a cure. Electra replies that the 'rite' which she seeks is death at the hands of Orestes, and only then will her dreams cease. Electra's vision of the murder is of a pursuit into the darkest recesses of the palace, where Orestes will track her with his torch. Hofmannsthal was, however, aware that the theme of ancient guilt is pervasive in Greek tragedy.

Electra may play the part of a psychoanalyst in her scene with her mother, but she also has psychological problems of her own. Her name was believed by Greek authors to mean 'unmarried', and this was regarded as a psychologically dangerous state for an adult woman (cf. Chapter 5 n. 5). Hofmannsthal develops these implications of the myth. Electra is traumatized by the death of her father, has a bad relationship with her mother, and shows repeated evidence of disturbed sexuality. She dwells obsessively on the past, and lives only for the moment of revenge. On the other hand, memory has an ethical as well a neurotic quality. Electra is repeatedly compared to animals, but also insists that it is memory that distinguishes human beings from beasts. A powerful speech in her scene with Orestes recalls the moral dilemma of her Sophoclean counterpart: 'All that I was I have / had to surrender. Even my shame which is / sweeter than all, which like the milky / silvery haze around the moon envelops / every woman and which turns infamy away / from her and her soul!'. Hofmannsthal, like Sophocles, was fascinated by the heroic obstinacy which refuses to compromise or forget.

Richard Strauss' *Elektra* (1909)

Richard Strauss (1864-1949) met Hofmannsthal for the first time in Berlin in 1899, and saw *Elektra* there in the autumn of 1905. He immediately recognized its potential as an operatic libretto. *Elektra* was the fourth of his fifteen operas, and the first of six collaborations with Hofmannsthal. He had been known primarily as a composer of tone poems and songs until the success of his previous opera *Salome* (1905), to which *Elektra* has striking if superficial similarities. Strauss was indeed inspired in both cases by plays produced by Reinhardt with Eysoldt in the title role. The première in Dresden on 25 January 1909 divided critical opinion, both because of the extreme nature of the text and because of conflicting views of the merits of Strauss' music.

Strauss adapted Hofmannsthal's text himself, so there was little actual collaboration on this occasion. Strauss reduced the text by one third. This was partly a matter of streamlining the action, but also involved some simplification of Hofmannsthal's complex psychology. Much could be left for the music to express.

Strauss' interventions already show the practical sense of what would work in the theatre which would recur throughout their collaboration. One example of his strong views on dramatic issues was his refusal to accept Hofmannsthal's suggestion that Aegisthus be left out altogether. Hofmannsthal had once even thought of leaving out Orestes, evidence that his interest in the three main female characters was even more exclusive than Sophocles'. Hofmannsthal's main contribution to was to add two short pieces of text. Strauss wanted a few more lines to emphasize Electra's ecstasy after her recognition of Orestes, before she moves on to speak in more sombre tones of the beauty which she has sacrificed. The second addition was again designed to emphasize Electra's joy, this time her celebration of the revenge. Hofmannsthal's play did not need text at this point, but Strauss found his finale rather abrupt for operatic purposes.

The symmetrical structure of Hofmannsthal's play gave Strauss the basis for a one-act opera in seven sections. He was able, as in *Salome*, to exploit the structure of the tone-poems in which he had specialized between 1889 and 1903. The opera is divided, after the Clytemnestra scene, into two halves of roughly equal duration. Elements of symphonic recapitulation have been detected in the second half of the opera, further emphasizing its formal cohesion. Chrysothemis is an even more positive figure than in Hofmannsthal, which leads to some dramatic problems in her first scene. Arnold Whittall writes: 'Strauss's E flat major music conveys too little of her sheer desperation. It has ample rhythmic energy, but insufficient harmonic flexibility, as if it is meant to depict the joys of motherhood as Chrysothemis imagines them, rather than her actual frustration at being denied them.'[9] Strauss' omission of two pages of Hofmannsthal's dialogue means that there is a drastic gear-change when Chrysothemis bursts into tears immediately after her passionate 'ich bin ein Weib und will ein Weiberschicksal' ('I am a woman and want a woman's lot'). Clytemnestra is a mezzo-soprano, often taken by older singers (Ernestine Schumann-Heink, who created the role, was 47).

William Mann observes: 'Strauss, after many performances' experience, thought it well to point out that she is not an ancient hag, but a proud and beautiful woman of about fifty whose ruin is primarily spiritual.'[10] Aegisthus, cast for a tenor, is provided with some undignified music and his appearance provokes satirical commentary from the orchestra. Orestes' baritone makes a remarkable impact after the predominance of female voices in the earlier part of the opera. Hofmannsthal's stage direction for his entrance was quoted above, and Strauss accompanies his opening words with a solemn D minor chord progression for Wagner tubas and trombones which suggests a supernatural aspect to his mission.

Hofmannsthal's Chrysothemis enters from the palace after the death of Aegisthus to report the celebrations inside, which are also to some extent audible and visible. Electra replies: 'I know very well that they are waiting for me, / because I must lead the dance.' She does not join the celebrations of the others, but starts a dance of her own: 'Be silent and dance. All must / approach! Here join behind me! I bear the burden / of happiness, and I dance before you.' Hofmannsthal may have been inspired by the chorus' exhortation to Euripides' Electra after the death of Aegisthus: 'Join in the dance, dear friend, leaping nimbly into the air like a fawn in celebration' (Euripides, *Electra* 859-61). Euripides' chorus dances, but Electra does not join it. Hofmannsthal seems to have distinguished two types of ancient Greek dance: the round dance ('Reigen'), which is communal and harmonious; and the solo maenadic dance. Bryan Gilliam has argued that Strauss associates these two types of dance with two distinctive keys, C major and E major respectively. E major, regularly associated in Strauss with extreme joy, is thus the key of Electra's dance.[11]

Electra's death is characterized by a quiet chord in E flat minor, which then alternates with fortissimo repetitions in C minor of the anapaestic (di-di-dum) motif associated with Agamemnon. Chrysothemis beats on the door of the palace and calls out for Orestes. The Agamemnon motif is transformed into a triumphant and harmonious C major in the last four bars of the opera, but the concluding C major chord is immediately preceded by the chord in E flat minor which is associated with Electra's death. The opera may end in triumph, but the exact nature of that triumph is open to question and darker elements persist into the very last bar.[12]

Electra in the twentieth century

Hofmannsthal and Strauss created the definitive *Electra* for the twentieth century, and later versions have struggled to escape from its shadow. This seems particularly to have been the case in Germany, where relatively infrequent performances are recorded in Helmut Flashar's comprehensive study of Greek drama on the modern stage. Flashar does, however, list no fewer than four productions in Germany in 1941 (in Munich, Guben, Göttingen, and Düren). This was part of a general interest in reviving Greek tragedy in the early years of the Second World War, when audiences were evidently attracted by dramas of heroic struggle and suffering.[13] In post-war Germany, a leading figure in staging Greek tragedy was Gustav Rudolf Sellner (1905-90), who directed an *Electra* in Darmstadt in 1956. Sellner worked closely with the distinguished classical scholar Wolfgang Schadewaldt (1900-74), who supplied the translation. Sellner seems to have favoured a stylized and ritualistic mode of performance, with careful choreography of the movements both of the chorus and of the actors. The effect of remoteness from everyday life was reinforced by the use of half-masks. Sellner wanted to emphasize the universal significance of the drama, focussing above all on the language. He later included *Electra* in a cycle of Greek tragedies at the Burgtheater in Vienna (1963), but seems to have been constrained by a wooden translation and an over-assertive stage-designer. A very different style was adopted by Roberto Ciulli in a production in Mühlheim in 1983, treating the play in terms of the theatre of the absurd. Flashar remarks that the tone was closer to Samuel Beckett than to Sophocles.

Electra has retained a prominent place in the repertoire in

Greece.[14] It was the play which in 1936 inaugurated a week of ancient Greek drama in the Herodes Atticus theatre in Athens, which had not been used for professional performances since an *Antigone* in 1867. The play was directed by Dimitris Rondiris (1899-1981), who was near the beginning of his two periods as director of the National Theatre (1934-42, 1946-50). Rondiris had worked with Max Reinhardt, and adopted from him the use of a large chorus with elaborate choreography. Electra was played by the celebrated Katina Paxinou (1900-73). Rondiris believed that a performance of an ancient tragedy should be a special spiritual event, to be distinguished from the regular repertoire, and that this effect could best be achieved in the ancient outdoor theatres. *Electra* was again the play when Rondiris directed the first modern performance in the theatre at Epidaurus on 11 September 1938. The performance took place in daylight, before an audience of 3,500. Paxinou again played the title role, but may have struggled to contend with the sixty-strong chorus. Rondiris brought *Electra* to London the following year, and on a tour of the United States and Canada in 1952 (still with Paxinou as Electra). The chorus remained a prominent feature of his productions. In 1957, he formed his own company, the Piraikon Theatron, with which he toured not only Greece but also Europe and the United States. The company brought *Electra* to London and New York in 1961 (with Aspasia Papathanasiou), with notable success in both cities. The company continued to take *Electra* on tour, including New York again in 1964 and the Edinburgh festival in 1966 (with Elsa Vergi now as Electra). Rondiris had evidently found a style which could communicate the power of the play internationally, even to audiences unfamiliar with modern Greek.[15]

A very different style marked a performance in Athens in November 1939, before an audience including the dictator Ioannis Metaxas. This featured the great actress Marika Kotopouli (1887-1953), and was directed by Karolos Koun (1908-87). Metaxas had been known to take offence at performances of ancient tragedies which implied criticism of tyranny, and had even censored Pericles' funeral speech (Thucydides 2.35-47).

This performance, however, seems principally to have been a celebration of Kotopouli's long career and of the theatre named after her. Koun's production was evidently on a less grandiose scale than those of Rondiris, in which the director was paramount, and focussed more on the individual characters and especially on Electra herself. *Electra*, like Euripides' *Medea*, has one of the great roles for a star actress, and this is one reason for its continuing success on the stage.

Electra did have a political resonance in the National Theatre production which opened at Epidaurus on 9 July 1972, directed by Spyros Evangelatos (1940-) and with Antigoni Valakou in the title role. Greece was ruled at the time by a military dictatorship ('the colonels') which imposed censorship on the theatre. Electra's resistance to a tyrannical régime was perceived to have topical significance, although Evangelatos prudently insisted on the authenticity of his production. This significance could be expressed more openly three years later, after the restoration of democracy, when the play was performed at Epidaurus under the direction of Minos Volanakis (1925-99), with Anna Synodinou (1927-) as Electra. One reviewer wrote: 'Mr Volanakis has taken Electra out of the house of Atreus and made her a symbol of a person who fights for her freedom against tyranny and violence .... As the lights went down the audience breathed an air of freedom. We experienced catharsis from the tyranny we as a nation have suffered too.'[16]

In the United States, Rondiris' touring productions are the only performances of *Electra* between 1932 and 1964 mentioned by Karelisa Hartigan in her study of Greek tragedy in the American commercial theatre.[17] In the earlier years of the twentieth century, however, the play was championed by two remarkable performers. The first of these was the Canadian actress-manager Margaret Anglin (1876-1958), who included a number of Greek tragedies in her touring repertoire between 1915 and 1928. She directed the plays herself, and was evidently the centre of attention. A performance of *Electra* in Carnegie Hall in February 1918 seems to have been a particular triumph, despite some concern about the subject matter of the play. Anglin's production had incidental music by Walter Damrosch (1862-1950), a leading figure in the New York musical life of the time. In May 1927, Anglin filled the Metropolitan Opera House for two further performances of *Electra*, but found the strain of the role too much to undertake a longer run. She seems to have had a grand style of tragic acting, which was regarded as suitable both to the play itself and to performance in large venues.

Anglin's grandeur contrasted markedly with the style of Blanche Yurka (?1887-1974), who played Electra in Boston in May 1931, and then in New York in January of the following year. Yurka had played a number of Ibsen roles in the later 1920s, and seems to have taken a more realistic and humanized approach to the play. Critics thought this more appropriate to Euripides, and compared it unfavourably with Anglin's elevated style. This problem of style may be the reason why Karelisa Hartigan finds no indigenous productions of *Electra* to discuss until 1964, when it featured in Joseph Papp's New York Shakespeare Festival at the Delacorte Theatre in Central Park, with Lee Grant (Electra) and Olympia Dukakis (Chrysothemis). The outdoor setting and popular audience, at least, established a link with the ancient Greek theatre. Productions of *Electra* in the United States since the 1960s seem not to have been restricted by idealized notions of classical style, and the play has been updated and adapted in a variety of ways to give it more immediate contemporary relevance.

Edith Hall remarks (p. 298) that the overwhelming impact of Strauss' opera may be a reason why *Electra* has been relatively little seen on the British stage in the twentieth century. A notable exception was the appearance of Peggy Ashcroft (1907-91) in a production at the Old Vic in London in 1951. This was evidently a production which revolved around the virtuosity and emotional power of the leading actress. The same was true of Deborah Warner's production for the Royal Shakespeare Company at the Barbican Theatre in London in 1989, using the translation by Kenneth McLeish, in which the title role was played by Fiona Shaw. The production did, however, acquire political relevance when it was revived for a tour in 1991/2. The tour included a series of performances in the Templemore Sport Stadium, Derry, 5-8 February 1992. This coincided with a particularly vicious phase of the conflict in Northern Ireland, in which sectarian vendetta-killings were taking place in Derry and elsewhere in the very week of the performances. Deborah Warner comments on the reaction to the play there: 'What happened for us was that because the thing was not being named, that audience in Derry was free imaginatively to map their entire lives against the play and that situation. That was very startling and terribly unexpected for us. We knew to a degree by then about the power of the performance, but that was unexpected. And at the end, they didn't clap: they wanted to talk about revenge instead, because they were very troubled about the notion of revenge.'[18] A notable feature of the conflict in Northern Ireland has been the political exploitation of funerals, not least in order to incite revenge, and it is not surprising that *Electra* should have seemed especially relevant.[19]

Irish dramatists may not have taken as much interest in *Electra* as in *Antigone*, but there has been a recent version by Frank McGuinness (1953-). McGuinness, who does not know Greek, based his play on two nineteenth-century translations. It had its première at Chichester in 1997, directed by David Leveaux and with Zoë Wanamaker as Electra. It was then performed with great success in London and New York. Electra in this production wore a man's heavy overcoat, recalling the disturbed and defeminized protagonist of McGuinness' earlier play *Baglady* (1985). Leveaux's production suggested a setting in Bosnia, but McGuinness has said that the conflict which he actually had in mind when writing the play was that in Northern Ireland. He insists, however, that the meaning of his play should not be confined to this: 'In the hinterland of my mind, the Northern conflict was there, but I did not want the play to be looked on as some kind of veiled metaphor for the civil war in the North of Ireland.'[20] McGuinness also found a more personal significance in the play. He remarks that both he and Zoë Wanamaker had lost a parent within six months of starting work on the play, and that their mourning informed their work on it. Fiona Shaw has drawn attention to the importance for her performance of Electra of the death of her eighteen-year-old brother in a car crash. We are taken back to the anecdote about the actor Polus in the fourth century BC. Mere acting does not seem adequate to express the force of Electra's grief.

Notes

1. Sophocles and his Theatre

1. A.W. Pickard-Cambridge, *The Dramatic Festivals of Athens* (2nd edn, revised by J. Gould & D.M. Lewis; Oxford: Oxford University Press, 1988), 58. The ancient evidence for the organization of the City Dionysia is translated, with a helpful introduction, in E. Csapo & W.J. Slater, *The Context of Ancient Drama* (Ann Arbor: University of Michigan Press, 1995), 103-21.

2. E.g. R. Rehm, *Greek Tragic Theatre* (London & New York: Routledge, 1992), 14-16. For a sceptical view, with references to earlier discussions, see P.J. Rhodes, 'Nothing to do with democracy: Athenian drama and the *polis*', *Journal of Hellenic Studies* 123 (2003), 104-19.

3. There is a brief but memorable account of Dionysus in W. Burkert, *Greek Religion* (Eng. tr. of German original published in 1977; Oxford: Blackwell, 1985), 161-7. For a judicious discussion of the 'Dionysiac' qualities of tragedy, see P.E. Easterling, 'A show for Dionysus', in P.E. Easterling (ed.), *The Cambridge Companion to Greek Tragedy* (Cambridge: Cambridge University Press, 1997), 36-53. For more sceptical views, see R. Friedrich, 'Everything to do with Dionysos? Ritualism, the Dionysiac, and the tragic', in M.S. Silk (ed.) *Tragedy and the Tragic* (Oxford: Oxford University Press, 1996), 257-83 (followed by a response by R. Seaford, pp. 284-94); S. Scullion, ' "Nothing to do with Dionysus": tragedy misconceived as ritual', *Classical Quarterly* 52 (2002), 102-37.

4. E.g. S.D. Goldhill, 'Representing democracy: women at the Great Dionysia', in R. Osborne & S. Hornblower (eds), *Ritual, Finance, Politics* (Oxford: Oxford University Press, 1994), 347-67; A.H. Sommerstein, 'The theatre audience, the *demos*, and the *Suppliants* of Aeschylus', in C.B.R. Pelling (ed.), *Greek Tragedy and the Historian* (Oxford: Oxford University Press, 1997), 63-79.

5. Recent scholars have tended to stress the specifically Athenian context of tragedy, in contrast to Aristotle's treatment of the plays as universal masterpieces which transcend the time and place of their original performance. See especially J.-P. Vernant & P. Vidal-Naquet, *Myth and Tragedy in Ancient Greece* (Eng. tr. of French originals published in 1972 and 1986; New York: Zone Books, 1988). See also

J.J. Winkler & F.I. Zeitlin (eds), *Nothing to Do with Dionysos? Athenian Drama in its Social Context* (Princeton: Princeton University Press, 1990). For a more sceptical view, see J. Griffin, 'The social function of Attic tragedy', *Classical Quarterly* 48 (1998), 39-61.

6. For a lively account of the staging of tragedy in Athens, with good illustrations, see O. Taplin, *Greek Tragedy in Action* (London: Methuen, 1978).

7. The distinction between mythical and historical tragedy is by no means clear-cut. See D.J. Conacher, *Aeschylus: The Earlier Plays and Related Studies* (Toronto: University of Toronto Press, 1996), 3-8. Cf. E. Hall (ed.), *Aeschylus:* Persians (Warminster: Aris and Phillips, 1996), 5-10.

8. Mark Griffith has recently developed the perhaps surprising view that Athenian tragedy consistently validates the authority of an aristocratic élite. Lower-class characters are repeatedly shown to be ineffectual and small-minded, and to depend on their betters for salvation and protection. Royal power may be problematized, he argues, but is never itself questioned. Xerxes (*Persians*) and Creon (*Antigone*) are unsatisfactory kings who are reduced to despair, but it would be unthinkable for their monarchy to be overthrown. See his edition of Sophocles' *Antigone* (Cambridge: Cambridge University Press, 1999), 54-8, with references to his earlier work on the subject.

9. See (e.g.) F.I. Zeitlin, *Playing the Other: Gender and Society in Classical Greek Literature* (Chicago & London: University of Chicago Press, 1996); E. Hall, 'The sociology of Athenian tragedy', in P.E. Easterling (ed.), *The Cambridge Companion to Greek Tragedy* (Cambridge: Cambridge University Press, 1997), 93-126; H.P. Foley, *Female Acts in Greek Tragedy* (Princeton & Oxford: Princeton University Press, 2001).

10. See M.R. Lefkowitz, *The Lives of the Greek Poets* (London: Duckworth, 1981), which includes a translation of the *Life of Sophocles* (pp. 160-3). There is an excerpt from the *Life*, together with other evidence for Sophocles' career (including the Ion anecdote mentioned below), in A.H. Sommerstein, *Greek Drama and Dramatists* (London & New York: Routledge, 2002), 161-3.

11. This story is discussed by A. Connolly, 'Was Sophocles heroized as Dexion?', *Journal of Hellenic Studies* 118 (1998), 1-21.

12. For an entertaining discussion of the effect of idealizing views of Sophocles on the interpretation of *Electra*, see M. Davies, ' "Leaving out the Erinyes": the history of a misconception', *Prometheus* 25 (1999), 117-28. Davies traces this line of interpretation back to the German philosopher A.W. Schlegel (1767-1845), and his influential *A Course of Lectures on Dramatic Art and Literature* (1809-11; tr. J. Black; London: H.G. Bohn, 1846).

2. The Story before Sophocles

1. Translations from the *Odyssey* are taken from the version by W.H. Shewring (Oxford: Oxford University Press, 1980).

2. See J. Griffin, 'The epic cycle and the uniqueness of Homer', *Journal of Hellenic Studies* 97 (1977), 39-53, at 44; reprinted in D.L. Cairns (ed.), *Oxford Readings in Homer's* Iliad (Oxford: Oxford University Press, 2001), 365-84, at 375. Cf. R. Seaford, *Reciprocity and Ritual* (Oxford: Oxford University Press, 1994), 11-13.

3. See generally J.F. Davidson, 'Homer and Sophocles' *Electra*', *Bulletin of the Institute of Classical Studies* 35 (1988), 45-72.

4. This translation is taken from M.L. West (ed.), *Greek Epic Fragments* (Loeb Classical Library, 497; Cambridge, Mass. & London: Harvard University Press, 2003), 75.

5. The fragments of Stesichorus' *Oresteia* (frr. 210-19) can be found, with English translation, in D.A. Campbell (ed.), *Greek Lyric*, vol. 3 (Loeb Classical Library, 476; Cambridge, Mass. & London: Harvard University Press, 1991), 126-33. There is a good discussion in A.F. Garvie (ed.), *Aeschylus:* Choephori (Oxford: Oxford University Press, 1986), xvii-xxiv.

6. The Furies are more properly termed Erinyes (sing. Erinys) in Greek, but the more familiar term is used here. The Erinyes punished violations of justice and of the natural order generally, and were especially concerned with offences within the family.

7. This translation is taken from W.H. Race (ed.), *Pindar: Olympian Odes, Pythian Odes* (Loeb Classical Library, 56; Cambridge, Mass. & London: Harvard University Press, 1997), 371.

8. See A.J.N.W. Prag, *The Oresteia: Iconographic and Narrative Tradition* (Warminster: Aris & Phillips, 1985); T.H. Carpenter, *Art and Myth in Ancient Greece* (London, 1991), 236-7, with illustrations 350-6. There are detailed and well-illustrated entries for the main characters in the *Lexicon Iconographicum Mythologiae Classicae* (Zurich & Munich: Artemis, 1981-97).

9. See Garvie (above, n. 5), xv.

10. On the much-discussed question of Clytemnestra's murder weapon (axe or sword), see Cropp's note on Euripides, *Electra* 160 and Garvie's note on Aeschylus' *Choephori* (= *Libation Bearers*) 889.

11. This translation is taken from the version by C. Collard (Oxford: Oxford University Press, 2002).

12. Revivals and school texts: A.H. Sommerstein (ed.), *Aristophanes: Frogs* (Warminster: Aris & Phillips, 1996), note on line 868. Euripides' *Electra*: Cropp, p. xlvi (cf. his index s.v. 'Aeschylus' for reference to specific points). *Phoenician Women*: see D.J. Mastronarde (ed.), *Euripides: Phoenissae* (Cambridge: Cambridge University Press,

1994), index s.v. 'Aeschylus'. Old comedy: K.J. Dover (ed.), *Aristophanes: Frogs* (Oxford: Oxford University Press, 1993), 23 n. 37; cf. A.H. Sommerstein, *Indexes* [to his commentaries on the plays of Aristophanes] (Warminster: Aris & Phillips, 2002), 4-8.
13. Cropp, pp. l-li. For a comparison of Euripides' *Electra* with Sophocles' *Electra*, see Cropp, pp. xlviii-xlix (and his index s.v. 'Sophocles' for reference to specific points).

3. The Action of the Play

1. Cf. D. Konstan, *Friendship in the Classical World* (Cambridge: Cambridge University Press, 1997).
2. A.M. Dale (ed.), *Euripides: Alcestis* (Oxford: Oxford University Press, 1954), note on lines 280 ff. The metre of the spoken parts of tragedy is mostly the iambic trimeter, which contrasts with the 'lyric', or sung, passages.
3. Cf. M.A. Lloyd, *The Agon in Euripides* (Oxford: Oxford University Press, 1992), 17, 101.
4. Cf. R. Thomas, *Herodotus in Context* (Cambridge: Cambridge University Press, 2000), 168-212, esp. 191-7.
5. The phrase which is translated as 'overcoming dishonour' is highly controversial, but must in the context be complimentary. See March's note on lines 1087-8; also Burton, pp. 213-14, MacLeod, pp. 148-52. Note that Lloyd-Jones prints a somewhat different text, which he translates 'giving a weapon to a noble remedy'.
6. F. Solmsen, 'Electra and Orestes: three recognitions in Greek tragedy', *Mededelingen der Koninklijke Nederlandse Akademie van Wetenschappen*, 30.2 (Amsterdam, 1967), 31-62, at 54-5.
7. Cf. A.M. Dale (ed.), *Euripides: Helen* (Oxford: Oxford University Press, 1967), note on lines 625-97.

4. Stagecraft

1. P.E. Easterling, 'Women in tragic space', *Bulletin of the Institute of Classical Studies* 34 (1987), 15-26, at 19-20. Cf. F. Budelmann, *The Language of Sophocles* (Cambridge: Cambridge University Press, 2000), 246-51.
2. B.M.W. Knox, 'Sophocles and the *polis*', *Entretiens Hardt* 29 (1983), 1-27, at 8. Contrast M.W. Blundell, *Helping Friends and Harming Enemies: A Study in Sophocles and Greek Ethics* (Cambridge: Cambridge University Press, 1989), 154-5.
3. Cf. Budelmann, pp. 257-9, with references.
4. J. Griffin, 'Sophocles and the democratic city', in J. Griffin (ed.), *Sophocles Revisited* (Oxford: Oxford University Press, 1999), 73-94, at 78-9.

5. C.P. Segal, 'The *Electra* of Sophocles', *Transactions of the American Philological Association* 97 (1966), 473-545, at 513.

6. R.B. Rutherford (ed.), *Homer: Odyssey Books XIX and XX* (Cambridge: Cambridge University Press, 1992), 71. See generally C. Gill & T.P. Wiseman (eds), *Lies and Fiction in the Ancient World* (Exeter: University of Exeter Press, 1993); J. Hesk, *Deception and Democracy in Classical Athens* (Cambridge: Cambridge University Press, 2000).

7. I.J.F. de Jong, *Narrative in Drama: The Art of the Euripidean Messenger-Speech* (Mnemosyne Supplement 116; Leiden: Brill, 1991).

8. J. Barrett, *Staged Narrative: Poetics and the Messenger in Greek Tragedy* (Berkeley, Los Angeles & London: University of California Press, 2002), esp. 160-7.

9. B. Vickers, *Towards Greek Tragedy* (London: Longman, 1973), 570.

10. C. Segal, *Interpreting Greek Tragedy* (Ithaca & London: Cornell University Press, 1986), 128.

11. The issues have been much discussed in recent years. See especially J. Gould, *Myth, Ritual, Memory, and Exchange: Essays in Greek Literature and Culture* (Oxford: Oxford University Press, 2001), 378-404; P.E. Easterling, 'Form and performance', in P.E. Easterling (ed.), *The Cambridge Companion to Greek Tragedy* (Cambridge, 1997), 151-77; D.J. Mastronarde, 'Knowledge and authority in the choral voice of Euripidean tragedy', *Syllecta Classica* 10 (1999), 87-104.

12. 'I can find no fault' is an emendation by the nineteenth-century German scholar C.G.A. Erfurdt, which is rightly accepted by most modern editors. The manuscript reading does not make sense.

5. Electra

1. E.g. G.M. Kirkwood, *A Study of Sophoclean Drama* (Ithaca: Cornell University Press, 1958), 34-6, 135-43; J. Griffin, 'Sophocles and the democratic city', in J. Griffin (ed.), *Sophocles Revisited* (Oxford: Oxford University Press, 1999), 73-94, at 78-82.

2. E.g. P.E. Easterling, 'Character in Sophocles', *Greece and Rome* 24 (1977), 121-9; reprinted in I. McAuslan & P. Walcot (eds), *Greek Tragedy* (Greece & Rome Studies, 2; Oxford: Oxford University Press, 1993), 58-65; J. Gould, *Myth, Ritual, Memory, and Exchange: Essays in Greek Literature and Culture* (Oxford: Oxford University Press, 2001), 78-111; C. Pelling (ed.), *Characterization and Individuality in Greek Literature* (Oxford: Oxford University Press, 1990).

3. A.F. Garvie (ed.), *Sophocles: Ajax* (Warminster: Aris & Phillips, 1998), 11.

4. Garvie (above, n. 3), 17. Cf. J. Hesk, *Sophocles: Ajax* (London: Duckworth, 2003), 59-60, 85-6, 136.

5. Cf. Jebb, pp. xix-xx. The motif of Electra's virginity is even more prominent in Euripides' *Electra* (cf. Cropp's note on line 44).

6. R. Seaford, 'The destruction of limits in Sophokles' *Elektra*', *Classical Quarterly* 35 (1985), 315-23. Cf. M. Alexiou, *The Ritual Lament in Greek Tradition* (Cambridge: Cambridge University Press, 1974).

7. R.C.T. Parker, *Miasma* (Oxford: Oxford University Press, 1983), 189. Cf. D.L. Cairns, *Aidôs: The Psychology and Ethics of Honour and Shame in Ancient Greek Literature* (Oxford: Oxford University Press, 1993). Cairns's discussion of *Electra* (pp. 241-9) is criticized by MacLeod, pp. 48-60.

8. B. Williams, *Shame and Necessity* (Berkeley, Los Angeles, & London: University of California Press, 1993), 84.

9. C. Gill, *Personality in Greek Epic, Tragedy, and Philosophy* (Oxford, 1996), 153; cf. his *Greek Thought* (Greece & Rome New Surveys in the Classics, 35; Oxford: Oxford University Press, 1995), 48.

10. A.M. van Erp Taalman Kip, 'Truth in tragedy: when are we entitled to doubt a character's words?', *American Journal of Philology* 117 (1996), 517-36, at 517.

11. Van Erp Taalman Kip (above, n. 10), 521.

12. B.M.W. Knox, 'The *Medea* of Euripides', *Yale Classical Studies* 25 (1977), 193-225, reprinted in *Word and Action* (Baltimore & London: The Johns Hopkins University Press, 1979), 295-322, and in E. Segal (ed.), *Oxford Readings in Greek Tragedy* (Oxford: Oxford University Press, 1983), 272-93, 440-4.

13. Cf. J.K. Campbell, *Honour, Family, and Patronage* (Oxford: Oxford University Press, 1964); J.A. Pitt-Rivers, *The Fate of Shechem* (Cambridge: Cambridge University Press, 1977).

14. Cf. G. Herman, 'Tribal and civic codes of behaviour in Lysias I', *Classical Quarterly* 43 (1993), 406-19; 'How violent was Athenian society?', in R. Osborne & S. Hornblower, *Ritual, Finance, Politics* (Oxford: Oxford University Press, 1994), 99-117. A balanced response to Herman is formulated by M. Schofield, in P. Cartledge, P. Millett, S. von Reden (eds), *Kosmos: Essays in Order, Conflict and Community in Classical Athens* (Cambridge: Cambridge University Press, 1998), 39 n. 5. Cf. R. Seaford, *Reciprocity and Ritual* (Oxford: Oxford University Press, 1994), 92-105, 198, 205, 216.

15. R. Just, *Women in Athenian Law and Life* (London & New York: Routledge, 1989), 153-4.

6. Matricide

1. J.T. Sheppard, 'The tragedy of Electra, according to Sophocles', *Classical Quarterly* 12 (1918), 80-8; '*Electra*: a defence of Sophocles',

Classical Review 41 (1927), 2-9; '*Electra* again', *Classical Review* 41 (1927), 163-5.

2. Stinton (pp. 238-9) discusses examples of expressions like 'if I am truly your son', where the speaker is confident of the identity of his father (e.g. Homer, *Odyssey* 9.529). Nevertheless, paternity could never be proved beyond all doubt in the days before DNA testing (e.g. Homer, *Odyssey* 1.215-16; Euripides, fr. 1015). On the inscrutability of the gods in Sophocles, see R.C.T. Parker, 'Through a glass darkly: Sophocles and the divine', in J. Griffin (ed.), *Sophocles Revisited* (Oxford: Oxford University Press, 1999), 11-30.

3. J.D. Denniston, *The Greek Particles* (2nd edn, Oxford: Oxford University Press, 1954), 451 remarks that 'much the commonest' use of the relevant particle (*goun*) is to introduce 'part proof' of a preceding statement. The 'emphatic' use cited by Stinton, pp. 478-9 (translating 'Yes, indeed: yours') is rare. Several of the examples of the 'emphatic' use cited by Denniston, p. 454 may really belong (as he says) in the 'part proof' category.

4. Sheppard, '*Electra*: a defence of Sophocles' (above, n. 1), 8.

5. D.H. Roberts, 'Sophoclean endings: another story', *Arethusa* 21 (1988), 177-96.

6. C. Thirlwall, 'On the irony of Sophocles', *Philological Museum* 2 (1833), 483-536; reprinted in R.D. Dawe (ed.), *Sophocles: The Classical Heritage* (New York & London: Garland, 1996), 179-223. Cf. G.M. Kirkwood, *A Study of Sophoclean Drama* (Ithaca: Cornell University Press, 1958), 247-87; D.C. Muecke, *The Compass of Irony* (London: Methuen, 1969); T.G. Rosenmeyer, 'Ironies in serious drama', in M.S. Silk (ed.), *Tragedy and the Tragic* (Oxford: Oxford University Press, 1996), 497-519.

7. A. & H. Paolucci (eds), *Hegel on Tragedy* (New York: Harper & Row, 1962), 325, from *Lectures on the Philosophy of Religion* (tr. E.B. Speirs & J.B. Sanderson; London: Routledge & Kegan Paul, 1968; translation first published 1895), ii. 264.

8. B. Vickers, *Towards Greek Tragedy* (London: Longman, 1973), 542.

9. E.g. Paolucci & Paolucci (above, n. 7), 176-8, from *The Philosophy of Fine Art* (tr. F.P.B. Osmaston; London: Bell, 1920), ii. 205-25.

10. O. Taplin, 'Comedy and the tragic', in M.S. Silk (ed.), *Tragedy and the Tragic* (Oxford: Oxford University Press, 1996), 188-202, at 197.

7. Afterlife

1. On the Greek acting profession, see E. Csapo & W.J. Slater, *The Context of Ancient Drama* (Ann Arbor: University of Michigan Press, 1995), 221-85; P.E. Easterling, 'From repertoire to canon', in P.E.

Easterling (ed.), *The Cambridge Companion to Greek Tragedy* (Cambridge: Cambridge University Press, 1997), 211-27; P.E. Easterling, 'Actor as icon', in P.E. Easterling & E. Hall (eds), *Greek and Roman Actors* (Cambridge: Cambridge University Press, 2002), 327-41.

2. The names of the main characters are, for convenience of comparison, rendered in this chapter in the same form as for Sophocles. Titles, however, are left in their original forms, as are the names of characters who do not appear in Sophocles.

3. The text of *Oreste* used here is that in *Les Œuvres Complètes de Voltaire*, 31A (Oxford: The Voltaire Foundation, 1992). The present discussion owes much to the exemplary introduction by the editor, David H. Jory.

4. Photographs of Eysoldt as Elektra are reproduced in S.D. Goldhill, *Who Needs Greek?* (Cambridge: Cambridge University Press, 2002), 155-7, plates 17-19 (see also the cover of the paperback edition).

5. The text of Hofmannsthal's *Elektra* used here is that in *Gesammelte Werke: Dramen II*, ed. H. Steiner (Frankfurt am Main: Fischer, 1954). English translations are taken from the version by Alfred Schwarz, in M. Hamburger (ed.), *Hugo von Hofmannsthal: Selected Plays and Libretti* (London: Routledge & Kegan Paul, 1963).

6. H.-J. Newiger, 'Hofmannsthals *Elektra* und die griechische Tragödie', *Arcadia* 4 (1969), 138-63, at 140-1, is adamant that Hofmannsthal did not know Euripides' *Electra* at this time. This would be rather surprising for someone with his knowledge of Greek drama, and is contradicted by several parallels between the two poets' presentation of Clytemnestra.

7. See H. Lloyd-Jones, 'Hofmannsthal's *Elektra* as a Goethean drama', *Publications of the English Goethe Society* 59 (1988-9), 16-34, reprinted in *Greek in a Cold Climate* (London: Duckworth, 1991); M. Davies, 'The three Electras: Strauss, Hofmannsthal, Sophocles, and the tragic vision', *Antike und Abendland* 45 (1999), 36-65.

8. See L. Martens, 'The theme of the repressed memory in Hofmannsthal's *Elektra*', *German Quarterly* 60 (1987), 38-51.

9. A. Whittall, 'Dramatic structure and tonal organisation', in D. Puffett (ed.), *Richard Strauss:* Elektra (Cambridge: Cambridge University Press, 1989), 55-73, at 62.

10. W. Mann, *Richard Strauss: A Critical Study of the Operas* (London: Cassell, 1964), 84. Mann also reproduces the useful diagram of the stage layout which Hofmannsthal supplied to Strauss (p. 71).

11. B. Gilliam, *Richard Strauss's* Elektra (Oxford: Oxford University Press, 1991), 223-35.

12. Goldhill (above, n. 4) devotes seventy pages to a discussion of the London première of Strauss' *Elektra* (19 February 1910), with barely a mention of the music.

13. H. Flashar, *Inszenierung der Antike: das griechische Drama auf*

der *Bühne der Neuzeit 1585-1990* (Munich: Beck, 1991), 169: 'Krieg, Sieg, Kampf und Leiden des Helden, die wartende Frau in der Heimat'. Flashar discusses other productions of *Electra* in Germany on 202-4 (Sellner) and 272-3 (Ciulli).

14. The main source for this section is Thalia Valeta, '*Electra* in Greece', *Didaskalia* 5.3 (2002). This article can be found in an issue of *Didaskalia* devoted to *Electra* (http://didaskalia.open.ac.uk/issues/vol5no3/contents.html). There is relevant material in P. Mavromoustakos, 'Medea in Greece', in E. Hall, F. Macintosh, & O. Taplin (eds), *Medea in Performance 1500-2000* (Oxford: Legenda, 2000), 166-79.

15. Films exist of performances of *Electra* at Epidaurus in 1938 and 1961 by the Greek National Theatre. They are briefly discussed by J.K. MacKinnon, *Greek Tragedy into Film* (London & Sydney: Croom Helm, 1986), 48-50. Orestes is played by the same actor, Thanos Kotsopoulos (1911-94), in both productions. There is a photograph of the 1938 production in D. Wiles, *Greek Theatre Performance: An Introduction* (Cambridge: Cambridge University Press, 2000), 121. Wiles (189-96) also discusses and illustrates three productions in differing styles by the French director Antoine Vitez (1966, 1971, 1986). MacKinnon (above, 60-3) discusses a film by Jean-Louis Ughetto (1972) of Vitez's 1971 production.

16. Quoted in her own translation by Valeta (above, n. 14). The writer is Stathis Dromazos. Hall, 264-75 discusses the use of *Electra* as political allegory in seventeenth- and eighteenth-century England. Wiles (above, n. 15), 192 quotes Antoine Vitez's account of the reception of his 1966 production in the newly-independent Algeria: 'The whole audience recognized in the *Electra* their nation humiliated for twenty-five years, subjected to colonial rule, restored to life when hope seemed lost.'

17. K.V. Hartigan, *Greek Tragedy on the American Stage* (Westport, CT: Greenwood Press, 1995), 25-35.

18. The quotation is taken from a discussion of the production by Deborah Warner and Fiona Shaw in the issue of *Didaskalia* cited above, n. 14. See also F. Shaw, 'Electra speechless', in F.M. Dunn (ed.), *Sophocles'* Electra *in Performance* (Stuttgart: M&P, 1996), 131-8. There is a photograph of the production in O. Taplin, *Greek Fire* (New York: Atheneum, 1990), 59. The Derry performances were reviewed by Mary Holland in the *Irish Times* (13 February 1992).

19. See F. Macintosh, *Dying Acts: Death in Ancient Greek and Modern Irish Tragic Drama* (Cork: Cork University Press, 1994), 30. This book has a photograph of Fiona Shaw as Electra on the cover.

20. See J. Long, 'The Sophoclean killing fields: an interview with

Frank McGuinness', in M. McDonald & J.M. Walton (eds), *Amid Our Troubles: Irish Versions of Greek Tragedy* (London: Methuen, 2002), 263-82, at 268. There is a photograph of Zoë Wanamaker as Electra in Hall, 299.

Guide to Further Reading

Translations

E.F. Watling, *Sophocles: Electra and Other Plays* (Harmondsworth: Penguin, 1953). Clear and vigorous translation, mostly in verse but with some passages in prose; very brief introduction and notes.

D. Grene, *Sophocles II* (in *The Complete Greek Tragedies*, ed. D. Grene & R. Lattimore; Chicago & London: University of Chicago Press, 1957). Verse translation, with brief introduction.

H.D.F. Kitto, *Sophocles: Antigone, Oedipus the King, Electra* (World's Classics series; Oxford: Oxford University Press, 1994 [first published 1962]. Verse translation, with introduction and notes by Edith Hall.

H. Lloyd-Jones, *Sophocles I: Ajax, Electra, Oedipus Tyrannus* (Loeb Classical Library, 20; Cambridge, Mass. & London: Harvard University Press, 1994). Brief introduction, reliable prose translation, and facing Greek text.

M. Ewans, *Sophocles: Three Dramas of Old Age* (Everyman Library; London: Dent, 2000). Fluent translation (designed for performance). Introduction and (40-page) running commentary focus on performance issues, and develop an idiosyncratic 'ironic' interpretation.

There is a translation of Aeschylus' *Oresteia*, with introduction and notes, by C. Collard (Oxford: Oxford University Press, 2002).

Commentaries

R.C. Jebb (Cambridge: Cambridge University Press, 1894). Introduction, Greek text, facing translation (dated, but often memorable), and detailed commentary. The basic resource for study of the play.

J.H. Kells (Cambridge: Cambridge University Press, 1973). Greek text, commentary, but no translation. Eccentric; supports an extreme 'ironic' interpretation.

J.C. Kamerbeek (Leiden: Brill, 1974). Introduction and commentary (in English), but no text or translation. There is an incisive review by D.A. Hester in *Mnemosyne* 28 (1975), 201-5, which criticizes

147

Kamerbeek's 'just but ugly' position and advocates an 'affirmative' interpretation.

J.R. March (Warminster: Aris & Phillips, 2001). Introduction, Greek text, facing translation, and commentary keyed to the translation. Useful format, but distorted by an extreme 'affirmative' interpretation.

There is much relevant to Sophocles' *Electra* in the excellent editions of Euripides' *Electra* (with translation) by M.J. Cropp (Warminster: Aris & Phillips, 1988), and of Aeschylus' *Choephori* [= *Libation Bearers*] by A.F. Garvie (Oxford: Oxford University Press, 1986).

Greek tragedy

E. Csapo & W.J. Slater, *The Context of Ancient Drama* (Ann Arbor: University of Michigan Press, 1995). Documents illustrating the ancient theatre.

P.E. Easterling & B.M.W. Knox (eds), *The Cambridge History of Classical Literature I: Greek Literature* (Cambridge: Cambridge University Press, 1985). The section on Greek drama is available separately in paperback. Informative discussions of tragedy in performance (J. Gould) and Sophocles (P.E. Easterling).

J. Gould, *Myth, Ritual, Memory, and Exchange: Essays in Greek Literature and Culture* (Oxford: Oxford University Press, 2001). Collection of articles dating from 1969 to 1999. Esp. relevant to *Electra* are chs 3 (character), 4 (women), 6 (performance), and 17 (chorus).

S. Hornblower & A. Spawforth (eds.), *The Oxford Classical Dictionary* (3rd edn; Oxford: Oxford University Press, 1996).

M.S. Silk (ed.), *Tragedy and the Tragic* (Oxford: Oxford University Press, 1996). The proceedings of a conference, giving a good impression of a range of modern responses to tragedy, even if there is little specifically on *Electra*.

E. Simon, *The Ancient Theatre* (London: Methuen, 1982; 1st German edn, 1972). Well-illustrated fifty-page introduction.

A.H. Sommerstein, *Greek Drama and Dramatists* (London & New York: Routledge, 2002). Introduction, including anthology of extracts.

O. Taplin, *The Stagecraft of Aeschylus* (Oxford: Oxford University Press, 1977). Includes much of relevance to Sophocles.

Books on Sophocles

M.W. Blundell, *Helping Friends and Harming Enemies: A Study in Sophocles and Greek Ethics* (Cambridge: Cambridge University

Press, 1989). Includes a subtle and detailed discussion of *Electra* in the light of Greek ethics.

F. Budelmann, *The Language of Sophocles* (Cambridge: Cambridge University Press, 2000). Broader than its title suggests, with some thoughtful pages on *Electra*.

R.W.B. Burton, *The Chorus in Sophocles' Tragedies* (Oxford: Oxford University Press,1980). Includes a forty-page chapter on the chorus in *Electra*.

B.M.W. Knox, *The Heroic Temper* (Berkeley & Los Angeles: University of California Press, 1964). Classic treatment of the Sophoclean hero, though with no chapter specifically on *Electra*.

L. MacLeod, *Dolos and Dike in Sophokles'* Elektra (Mnemosyne Supplement 219; Leiden: Brill, 2001). Useful especially for its balanced discussion of earlier scholars' views on the main issues in the play.

D. Seale, *Vision and Stagecraft in Sophocles* (London: Croom Helm, 1982). Includes a perceptive chapter on *Electra*.

C.P. Segal, *Tragedy and Civilization: An Interpretation of Sophocles* (Cambridge, Mass. & London: Harvard University Press, 1981). Structuralist; includes an eloquent statement of the 'just but ugly' interpretation of *Electra*.

R.P. Winnington-Ingram, *Sophocles: An Interpretation* (Cambridge: Cambridge University Press, 1980). The best general book on Sophocles; includes an 'ironic' interpretation of *Electra*.

Articles on *Electra*

H. Friis Johansen, 'Die Elektra des Sophokles', *Classica et Mediaevalia* 25 (1964), 8-32 (in German). Powerful statement of the corrupting effect of the revenge on Electra.

C.P. Segal, 'The *Electra* of Sophocles', *Transactions of the American Philological Association* 97 (1966), 473-545. Explores the negation of life by death in the play, with special reference to the character of Electra.

P.T. Stevens, 'Sophocles: *Electra*, doom or triumph?', *Greece and Rome* 25 (1978), 111-20. Brief statement of the 'affirmative' position.

T.C.W. Stinton, 'The scope and limits of allusion in Greek tragedy', in *Collected Papers on Greek Tragedy* (Oxford: Oxford University Press, 1990), 454-492. This article (first published in 1986) contains forceful criticisms of Winnington-Ingram, and a well-argued statement of the 'just but ugly' position (pp. 465-79).

T.A. Szlezák, 'Sophokles' *Elektra* und das Problem des ironischen Dramas', *Museum Helveticum* 38 (1981), 1-21 (in German). The best statement of the 'affirmative' position.

T.M. Woodard, '*Electra* by Sophocles: the dialectical design', *Harvard Studies in Classical Philology* 68 (1964), 163-205; 70 (1965), 195-

233. Detailed analysis, focussing on the contrast between *logos* (word) and *ergon* (deed), associated with Electra and Orestes respectively.

Afterlife

E. Hall, 'Sophocles' *Electra* in Britain', in J. Griffin (ed.), *Sophocles Revisited* (Oxford: Oxford University Press, 1999), 261-306. Lively and informative discussion; well-illustrated.

J.D. Reid (ed.), *The Oxford Guide to Classical Mythology in the Arts, 1300-1900s* (Oxford: Oxford University Press, 1993). The entry under 'Orestes' lists many modern versions of the myth, only some of which derive specifically from Sophocles' *Electra*.

The following two databases include information about modern performances and adaptations of *Electra*:

The Archive of Performances of Greek and Roman Drama (Oxford University)
http://www.apgrd.ox.ac.uk/

The Reception of the Texts and Images of Ancient Greece in Late Twentieth-Century Drama and Poetry in English (The Open University)
http://www2.open.ac.uk/ClassicalStudies/GreekPlays/

Chronology

All dates are BC.

c. 725: Homer's *Iliad*
c. 700: Homer's *Odyssey*

c. 534: Thespis wins first tragic competition in Athens
c. 525: Birth of Aeschylus
508/7: Beginning of democracy in Athens

c. 496: Birth of Sophocles
490: Battle of Marathon (Athenians defeat Persian expedition)
480: Battle of Salamis (Greeks defeat Persians)
c. 480: Birth of Euripides
472: Aeschylus' *Persians* (earliest surviving tragedy)
468: Sophocles' debut at the City Dionysia
458: Aeschylus' *Oresteia* (*Agamemnon, Libation Bearers, Eumenides*)
456: Death of Aeschylus
455: Euripides' debut at the City Dionysia
443/2: Sophocles *hellenotamias* (one of ten treasurers of Athenian empire)
?442: Sophocles' *Antigone*
441/0: Sophocles one of ten Athenian generals
431: Peloponnesian War begins
420: Sophocles receives cult of healing god Asclepius into Athens
c. 422-417: Euripides' *Electra*
?410s: Sophocles' *Electra* (not known if before or after Euripides' *Electra*)
415: Athenian expedition to Sicily (defeated 413)
413-11: Sophocles *proboulos* (one of ten emergency commissioners)
411: Athens ruled by oligarchy of the Four Hundred
409: Sophocles' *Philoctetes*
407/6: Death of Euripides
406/5: Death of Sophocles
405: Aristophanes' *Frogs*

151

404: Athens defeated by Sparta in Peloponnesian War
401: Sophocles' *Oedipus at Colonus* (produced posthumously)

Glossary

The meanings given here should be supplemented by the fuller explanations given in the text (see Index for references).

The suggestions about pronunciation in brackets are intended only to give a rough indication of how the words may be pronounced in an English context. They are not a technical guide to the authentic pronunciation of these words in Greek.

Agôn (ag-own). Formal debate.
Aidôs (eye-doze). Shame, respect.
Aischros (eye-skros). Shameful, ugly.
Anagnôrisis (an-ag-no-ri-sis). Recognition.
Antistrophê (an-tis-tro-fi). Stanza of lyric poetry.
Dolos (dolos). Cunning, treachery.
Eisodos (eye-sod-os). Side-entrance to stage.
Ekkyklêma (ecky-claimer). Trolley revealing interior scene.
Hybris (hibris). Wanton violence or injustice.
Kairos (kye-ros). What is appropriate, opportune, effective.
Kalos (kalos). Beautiful, fine, honourable.
Kleos (clay-os). Fame.
Parodos (par-od-os). First song of the chorus.
Pelopidae (Pel-opid-eye). Descendants of Pelops.
Philos (pl. *philoi*) (filos). Friend, loved one, relative.
Polis (polis). City-state.
Skênê (skay-nay). Stage building.
Sôphrôn (so-frone). Sensible, chaste, restrained.
Sôphrosunê (so-frozi-nay). Sense, chastity, self-restraint.
Stasimon (stas-im-on) . Song of the chorus.
Strophê (strow-fi). Stanza of lyric poetry.

Index

Index

157

Index

Index

Ughetto, J.-L. 145
urn 30, 54-7, 61-2, 70-1, 92, 118, 122

Valakou, A. 132
van Erp Taalman Kip, A.M. 86-7
Vergi, E. 131
Vickers, B. 70, 112
virginity 24, 81, 126-7
Vitez, A. 145
Volanakis, M. 132
Voltaire 117, 121-3

Wanamaker, Z. 134-5
Warner, D. 133-4
Whittall, A. 128
Wilde, O. 125
Williams, B.A.O. 83
Winnington-Ingram, R.P. 67, 69, 78, 87, 102-3, 104-5
women 11, 13, 38, 45, 51, 57, 73, 95-6, 103

Xanthus (poet) 23

Yurka, B. 133